I0422258

CELL
TOWER
SECRETS

Copyright 2025 by James Kennedy. All Rights Reserved.

No part of this publication may be reproduced, distributed, or transmitted in any form or by any means, including photocopying, recording, or other electronic or mechanical methods, without the prior written permission of the publisher, except in the case of brief quotations embodied in critical reviews and certain other noncommercial uses permitted by copyright law.

Although the author and publisher have made every effort to ensure the information in this book was correct at press time, neither the author nor publisher assumes and hereby disclaim any liability to any party for any loss, damage, or disruption caused by errors or omissions, whether such errors or omissions result from negligence, accident, or any other cause.

Adherence to all applicable laws and regulations, including international, federal, state, and local governing professional licensing, business practices, advertising, and all other aspects of doing business in the US, Canada, or any other jurisdiction, is the sole responsibility of the reader and consumer.

Neither the author nor the publisher assumes any responsibility or liability whatsoever on behalf of the consumer or reader of this material. Any perceived slight of any individual or organization is purely unintentional.

The resources in this book are provided for informational purposes only and should not be used to replace the specialized training and professional judgment of a tax, legal, or financial professional.

The information in *Cell Tower Secrets* should not be construed as tax, legal, or financial advice. It consists of information that is publicly available at the time of this writing. Those considering the sale of a cell tower lease or the purchase or sale of a property (with or without a cell tower lease) should obtain qualified professional tax, legal, and financial advice from a licensed accountant or attorney.

ISBN (Ebook): 979-8-88757-292-5

ISBN (Paperback): 979-8-89034-506-6

CELL
TOWER
SECRETS

Proven Cell Tower Lease Management
and Sales Strategies for Landlords
and Real Estate Professionals

TABLE OF CONTENTS

JAMES KENNEDY

CHAPTER 1
INTRODUCTION

After working with cell tower leases for many years, I was surprised to observe a distinct lack of single-source information regarding cell towers, cell tower leases, and the industry—especially as each relates to real estate. I have long believed a guide is needed to describe the cell tower industry. This guide should outline cell tower lease negotiation techniques, explain how cell tower lease values are determined and quantified, and unveil the idiosyncrasies cell towers and cell tower leases can impose on underlying and sometimes adjacent real estate.

I wrote this book to meet the need for information about the still burgeoning cell tower lease market and the art of cell tower-related deals. In this guide, I also cover the basics of the cell tower business from the landlord's perspective, paying careful attention to the above-mentioned considerations and associated technologies.

In reviewing the cell tower industry, I will also examine various purchase and sale considerations, the history of the cell tower market and its players, deal structures, financing concerns and opportunities, potential tax considerations, industry-specific clauses, suggestions for closing cell tower-related transactions properly and effectively, and the various infrastructure types. Regarding infrastructure, I'll also discuss utility company- and government-operated towers.

While this book should provide useful insights into the world of cell towers and cell tower leases, there is much more to understand. If one endeavors to successfully negotiate or effectively manage a cell tower-related property, there are many things to contemplate. Therefore, I urge landlords and property managers

1

to secure professional cell tower lease management advice or support when starting, especially if a cell tower lease transaction occurs with the purchase or sale of real estate.

Cell Tower Secrets is designed to clarify the issues a typical cell tower landlord may experience. It will be useful to most cell tower landlords because cell tower leases—while a small vertical relative to the entire real estate industry—represent a significant and under-managed component of hundreds of thousands of properties across the United States. In most scenarios, a cell tower lease can become a formidable and disproportionate value driver—if it is properly understood, negotiated, and managed.

WHO SHOULD READ THIS BOOK?

Whether you are new to real estate, a seasoned real estate veteran, a landlord, a government official, an investor, or a legal professional, *Cell Tower Secrets* provides no-nonsense advice about cell towers and cell tower leases. I will address many issues one should consider when incorporating such leases into or partitioning such leases from real estate investments.

You'll also gain insight into sector-specific elements of cell towers and cell tower leases that are beyond the scope of typical real estate transactions and traditional real estate management scenarios.

HOW TO USE THIS BOOK AND WHEN TO SEEK PROFESSIONAL ASSISTANCE

This book can be read from cover to cover as a step-by-step guide or selectively focusing on the material beneficial for a specific situation or scenario.

That said, it is not a substitute for qualified, professional advice. While recommendations about the need to consider retaining a competent and experienced cell tower lease consultant are scattered throughout *Cell Tower Secrets*, such recommendations do not imply that readers should contact the author (although the invitation is open).

The purpose of this book and its recommendations are three-fold:

- To educate interested parties about the finer points of cell towers, cell tower leases, and the cell tower industry.

- To educate cell tower landlords, real estate, and legal professionals about the ins and outs of the cell tower industry and common issues that arise while purchasing, selling, or managing properties subject to a cell tower or cell tower lease.

- To caution the reader against potential complications that may be best served by obtaining qualified, professional advice and to indicate the types of advice that should be sought (whether from an engineer, an attorney, a broker, or another professional with skills related to cell tower leases or infrastructure).

FREQUENTLY USED TERMS

The following terms may be used interchangeably (as appropriate) throughout this book:

1. Lessor, landlord, and property owner

2. Lessee, tenant, carrier, and tower company

3. Sub-tenant, sub-lessee, sub-licensee, and collocates (or colocates) may appear to be somewhat synonymous (as the right for a lessee, licensee, or tenant to lease to a third

party is common in cell tower leases and is often tied to collocation and revenue sharing)

4. The wireless telecommunications industry, cell tower industry, and the industry

As you read, you will come across several terms you may not have seen or heard previously. Some are technical, industry-specific, or terms of art. Sometimes, I'll use a term I've coined to refer to something specific. In those cases, I'll do my best to explain what those terms mean. For your convenience, I've included a glossary and two appendixes in the back of the book.

SUBJECTIVE NATURE AND DISCLAIMER

While portions of *Cell Tower Secrets* contain specific advice and quantifiable data, most of the content is based on my personal and professional experience. It includes my observations about cell towers and leases and how they relate to and impact the underlying and associated real estate.

Although I've never been an employee of any carrier or tower company, I've worked across the table with representatives from based entirely on my experiences with carrier and tower company actions, policies, and transactions from a landlord's or property manager's perspective. This includes the changes I've observed to cell tower lease-related variables and clauses and the wide variety of changes in the wireless telecommunications industry over the years. During the past twenty years, I've also analyzed and/or negotiated thousands of cell tower leases, including extensions and amendments.

Finally, I've studied the publicly traded carriers and tower companies at length. That includes their ongoing wireless technology rollouts and countless interactions with government agencies, including the FCC and various courts nationwide. I also regularly review industry-specific SEC filings and carrier and tower company financial and market data as they become available.

Cell Tower Secrets is intended to be a guide, not a bible. I do not claim nor intend to imply that my opinions and observations apply to every circumstance. Nor do I claim you will experience the same outcomes and observations described in this book.

That disclaimer aside, statements in this book are applicable in most situations relative to the examples discussed. However, every scenario is subject to exceptions based on various factors and should be viewed with that in mind.

CHAPTER 2
THE WIRELESS TELECOMMUNICATIONS
INDUSTRY: A PEEK BEHIND THE CURTAIN

I began exploring the wireless telecom industry purely by happenstance. I'd been studying cell towers for a couple of years. I had come across a few worthwhile cell tower-related deals when I stumbled across a listing for a small commercial property that included a cell tower with an active lease.

The property was a mess. The broker appeared to be somewhat uninformed, which surprised me. While I understood real estate and cell towers, I wasn't sure how to structure the potential deal.

The broker's name was Rich, an older gentleman, probably in his 60s. He said, "I've been selling real estate for forty years and can't give this damn thing away. Nobody seems to know what to do with it or how much it's worth."

I was a little surprised at Rich's blunt statement but chalked it up as part of the reason the property remained unsold. I said, "Rich, I like challenges. While I can't say I'm an expert at closing real estate transactions involving cell towers, I think I can put this deal together at the right price."

We exchanged information, and I learned what I could about the property and the cell tower lease to present an offer.

It took me a couple of days, but I put together the basic elements of the deal. That included who would buy the lease and the property, how to structure the transaction, the strong and weak points of the property as well as the lease in question, and how I hoped to close the deal.

After I did all that, I contacted Rich and arranged a meeting with him. It turned out that the property was listed as a part of an estate sale, and the heirs wanted nothing to do with it. I realized I enjoyed significant negotiating leverage thanks to Rich's willingness to overshare. I knew he hadn't succeeded in moving the property, even with multiple price reductions. I also observed that Rich wasn't knowledgeable about the cell tower lease market or how such a lease impacted his listing. And I now observed that the heirs to the estate for whom Rich worked were more than anxious to get rid of the property.

While asking Rich questions about the property condition, environmental issues, title, and the cell tower, he cut me off and exclaimed, "It's AS-IS, and there are NO disclosures!"

"Well, that makes my job easier," I replied. "The asking price is $995,000, and you've dropped it three times in the last year (the original asking price was $1,295,000). I guess the market has spoken." I promised I'd have an offer on Rich's table the following day.

For the remainder of the day, I gathered final offers on the lease and contacted several investor friends I thought might be interested in the property. Then, I pitched the deal as follows.

"The property is currently listed at $995,000, but I want to exclude the cell tower lease from the sale. Give me your best quick close, "as-is" cash offer for the property alone."

By the following day, I had four solid offers on the property and three more on the lease, which confirmed how much Rich misunderstood this property and the market.

When I met Rich again, I said, "I have good and bad news. Which do you want to hear first?"

"James," he pressed, "I just want to hear the news about the offer."

I focused my talking points specifically on the downsides. I discussed that the cell tower was poorly situated on the property. Not only was it unsightly, but it prevented any meaningful redevelopment of the property.

As I rattled off my concerns about the property, Rich chimed in. "James, I know everything you are telling me, but I still don't have your price. Please tell me your offer so I can present it to the sellers."

I paused for a second and said, "Before I share my proposed price and terms with you, I need you to agree that we will contact the sellers while I'm here to see if we have a deal. Okay?"

Rich agreed.

"My investors are prepared to give you $700,000 cash, assuming we receive a 3 percent credit back at closing instead of commission. We'd also like a 60-day contingency period and a 90-day close."

Rich paused momentarily and said, "If you had offered me that a few months ago, I'd have chased you out of here, but I think that might work today. Let's give the sellers a call."

To make a long story short, the sellers grudgingly agreed but insisted that we get everything executed that day. And we did.

I contacted the winning investor and told him the good news. He'd get the property without the lease for just under $600,000. Then, once we had it under contract, we'd complete the negotiations for selling the cell tower lease. It sold contemporaneously, with the property closing as a perpetual easement for just over $400,000.

The rest is history.

AN INTRODUCTION TO THE CELL TOWER INDUSTRY

If you purchase property that includes a cell tower, already have, or plan to manage or consult for others possessing such properties, it would benefit you to learn something about what you might expect to observe as a part of the process.

The wireless telecommunications industry can be as alarming as it is intriguing, as exciting as it is discouraging, and as precise as it is ambiguous. To put it another way, what sets the cell tower industry apart from other industries is its ability to remain eclectic while pushing the envelope on innovation. To sum it up, wireless telecom is both the vehicle and the driver of much of the personal technology we use daily, affecting us in ways we do not immediately realize.

CELL TOWER PROPERTY BENEFITS AND RESPONSIBILITIES

If you've been fortunate enough to own or manage a property on which a cell tower has been constructed and for which there is an *active* ground lease, you must become—or hire someone who is—a relative expert on what it means to be a cell tower lease landlord.

For starters, being a cell tower lease landlord is similar to being a landlord for other types of real estate, and in many respects, it *appears to be* simpler. That's largely because the typical wireless tenant rarely has a representative on-site. Once construction is complete—except for periodic maintenance, upgrades, repairs, or emergencies—cell tower tenants are among the most trouble-free and drama-free of real estate tenants. Most cell tower lease tenants also make timely payments, and the leases typically require the lessee to reimburse the lessor for a proportionate or segregated share of property expenses.

Being a cell tower lease landlord also means being largely free of loud, destructive, or disruptive tenants and their acquaintances.

Owning and operating property with an income-producing cell tower lease can also be lucrative (in some cases, it may subsidize most or all of the costs of property ownership). Even if a cell tower lease provides average market rent, it can be worth hundreds of thousands of dollars if monetized into a lump-sum single payment. An average cell tower lease may generate as much as a million dollars or more over the entire lease life cycle, but only if the cell tower lease is properly managed and isn't decommissioned early.

Cell tower leases may also represent unique monetization opportunities relative to other real estate leases. They often provide landlords with unparalleled security and flexibility when properly understood. Landlords also have the potential to sell or retain their cell tower leases independently of the fee-simple property on which a cell tower in question is constructed and operated. That is a rare quality among real estate leases.

An effective cell tower landlord or manager knows the limits, restrictions, and responsibilities imposed upon a property due to a cell tower and its lease. If one is already a cell tower landlord or manager, understanding these limits, restrictions, and responsibilities—if one does not already—should become a top priority.

Additionally, one should concern one's self with:

1. Examining prospective cell tower-related properties in greater detail;

2. Seeking out cell tower rents from other local landlords;

3. Monitoring the status of local, new cell site builds, and

4. Closely following new industry developments and legislative changes that may affect you and your site.

Finally, one must be well-organized regarding the tower and the lease while determining the essential negotiation points to max- imizing benefits and mitigating risks. Cell tower lease negotia- tions will likely become—if they haven't already—an ongoing and integral part of any cell tower lease landlord experience.

An introductory word of advice: Cell tower leases should not be managed as though they only provide "mailbox money." While carriers and tower companies prefer landlords who take a passive approach, remaining vigilant for the most unexpected and benevolent events is critical. The carriers and tower compa- nies will maintain their advantage for as long as a landlord ac- quiesces, which may ultimately cost the landlord in lost revenue and equity instead of maximizing each. I will discuss this topic at length throughout the book.

THE FOUNDING OF STEEPSTEEL

I learned a lot about the cell tower leasing industry during the years following my first cell tower-related real estate deal with Rich. I quickly became a specialist in locating and securing con- tracts for properties similar to that first cell tower property. My partnered investors and I created deals all around the country.

We obtained a variety of properties because of the cell tower leases. You name it; we encountered it: industrial, residential, of- fice, marina, rural, forest, R&D, shopping center, and even vacant land. Although the cell tower lease market had been around for a while, the inefficiencies I observed in the first transaction were commonplace in virtually every market and most all verticals, from coast to coast.

Most brokers are relatively uninformed about cell towers and cell tower leases, and—due to the industry's fragmented, disorganized, and complex nature—most are unmotivated to learn. Most also don't see enough cell tower-related properties in their local markets to consider the opportunities or to make it a point to learn more about the industry.

While the property we purchased through Rich was exciting, it took us some time to develop the skills necessary to maximize the values of the leases and the properties before *and* after closing. The IRRs consistently reached 30 percent or more once we developed the requisite skills.

After spending more than a decade in the industry working as an investor, manager, and consultant for clients with cell tower lease-related properties and transactions, I observed a significant need for professional assistance in the government and utility sectors. That's why I founded SteepSteel.

SteepSteel now provides consulting and management services to government agencies, utilities, corporations, private real estate companies and landlords, and non-profit landlords throughout the United States.

SteepSteel's focus has always been to provide superior service and advice to our clients, maximizing their cell tower lease and tower asset values while mitigating risks. In doing so, SteepSteel has flown under the radar to become one of the premier cell tower consulting and management firms in the United States.

THE CELL TOWER INDUSTRY: OPACITY AND COMPLEXITY

Most people don't consider the cell tower industry to be purely real estate. It isn't. If it was, every broker, real estate attorney, city manager, engineer, property manager, and appraiser around the country would have it all figured out, but they don't. Aside from private landlords, I still receive more calls from corporate and government real estate, legal, and engineering professionals than anyone else.

In many respects, the industry operates by a different set of rules than the rest of the real estate industry. From contracts (proprietary versus government) and the marketplace (hundreds of thousands of sites versus hundreds of millions of properties) to the data (proprietary and opaque versus public and transparent), the wireless telecommunications industry is often opposed to real estate in terms of function, understanding, and risk.

On any given day, a wide variety of highly competent real estate, legal, and management professionals around the country get duped while managing or negotiating a proposed or existing cell tower lease. In most instances, they are naively finessed into executing a lease, a lease amendment, a lease extension, or a lease sale document in exchange for what—in relative terms—would likely earn them peanuts in the short term. Plus, it would cost them a fortune in lost wireless asset equity and potential revenue that would not be recovered for years, if ever.

That's what carriers and tower companies have come to expect from most lessors and managers. A lack of readily available market data combined with an absence of widespread, long-term asset class experience appears to create a largely credulous lessor/manager mindset. This mindset also eliminates much of the scrutiny that might otherwise occur. Additionally, such circumstances virtually eliminate lessor discovery of potentially significant and beneficial upsides that *should be* captured *en masse.* Regrettably, once lost, such upsides are rarely realized.

In the right hands, such opportunities are seized promptly and often, creating significant lessor equity and mitigating risk that most often occurs exclusively at carrier or tower company expense (as it should be).

People often ask why the cell tower industry is so confusing. My response is somewhat blunt: "It's by design." That doesn't imply that carriers and tower companies have some dubious agenda. Rather, they prefer to keep information about their assets and agreements obscured from public view. Making such information public would do nothing to aid carriers and tower companies in maximizing their collective bottom lines or improving their on-going negotiations.

Unfortunately, that statement and its logic can appear disingenuous to those who don't know or understand the industry. Most people cannot fathom that the answer to an ostensibly simple question—"How much is my cell tower lease worth?"—can be complex and usually begins with the proverbial, "It depends..."

THE MYSTERIES AND OPPORTUNITIES OF THE CELL TOWER LEASE MARKET

As mentioned previously, if there were an improved understanding and comprehensive public access to centralized and verifiable real-time lease and tower data, the cell tower lease market and associated management would likely be much different. At a minimum, each would become more balanced and better understood.

As it stands, holding and managing cell tower leases is—albeit frequently perceived to be simpler—different from managing other real estate verticals. While managing cell tower leases bears many similarities to real estate management, don't be fooled by the apparent similarities to mean that cell towers and cell tower leases should be managed "like real estate."

VALUE DRIVERS

It is important to remember that cell tower lease values are not entirely based upon a given property's value or vice-versa. However, cell tower lease values and property values do impact each other. This is partially because cell towers are not necessarily placed on the "best property" or "best location" from a real estate perspective. What makes a superior location for a cell tower may not be the same as what makes a superior location for other types of real estate. After all, each property type's uses, objectives, and needs—while overlapping—are often quite different.

There are also concerns about the "highest and best use" of a property. Does having a cell tower on a property benefit the lessor as much as it would be if the area occupied by the tower and equipment were used for another purpose? One should consider whether the opportunity costs and appearance of the tower reduce the property's value more than the lease potentially increases it. I will discuss these issues more in Chapter 7 under the "Value Penalty" and "Lease Stripping" sections.

I'm not saying that a local real estate market cannot significantly affect a cell tower lease's equity value or rental rate. However, several other lease, site, or market-specific variables could impact the value of the rent or equity as much or more than the real estate itself. I will discuss these variables in Chapter 6: "Cell Tower Lease Valuation Variables."

This also means that cell tower lease valuation is less real estate-centric than commercial or residential real estate. For example, if one wants to know how much their cell tower lease is worth, CoStar, CREXI, Realtor.com, and Zillow won't help, nor will any local MLS. That means the estimated value will be based on research, expertise, analysis, and a lot of privately and publicly sourced data.

MARKET SAVVY

Because the cell tower industry is so opaque, the carriers and tower companies—which manage an immense amount of data and employ highly-trained and sharp employees & vendors—

typically hold enormous negotiating leverage relative to the average lessor. This fact is almost undisputed whether the lessor is private, corporate, government, or utility. Even if a lessor has access to the same or similar data as a carrier or tower company, the ability to analyze and develop viable and appropriate conclusions is another challenge altogether.

When one combines the opacity and complexity of the data with the limited supply of cell tower properties relative to all commercial and residential real estate, it's not difficult to see why few people bother to learn about the industry in general, let alone specific cell tower sites. Beyond that, one must become competent in the review of surveys, leases, deeds, easements, engineering reports, title reports, construction drawings, mapping locations, and legal descriptions. Additionally, one must have an in-depth understanding of discounted cashflows and the time value of money. An understanding of other advanced financial concepts also comes in handy.

Most importantly, one must understand cell tower lease lifecycles and the ever-changing carrier and tower company market compositions and maneuvers. These operate much like a deck of cards constantly reshuffled. Cell tower market players undergo major acquisitions, sales, mergers, developments, and network/technology enhancements.

Finally, one must pay close attention to legislative, geopolitical, and economic developments that may affect the wireless telecommunications industry. That's true whether they happen to be global (supply chain issues, emerging technologies, etc.), national (regulations, mergers, cost of capital, network development, taxation, etc.), state (transaction and finance laws), or local (zoning, restrictions, CUP's, etc.).

In short, there are so many variables in cell tower lease transactions that one cannot be too prepared.

CHAPTER 3
THE PLAYERS INVOLVED IN
THE CELL TOWER GAME

Having worked with most of the carriers, tower companies, and aggregators in the industry over the last twenty-something years, I will note that many people categorize experiences in the wireless telecommunications industry based on the company "type" (i.e., carrier, tower company, aggregator, optimizer, etc.). However, most of my experiences with companies in the industry have been positive and productive. That said, most people in the industry are savvy and should be approached with that in mind.

In this chapter, I'll summarize each type of company in the wireless telecom industry. I intend to give you an overview of the leading companies in the industry, cover the stated purpose of each type of company, and explain what such purposes may mean to a cell tower lease landlord.

CARRIERS AND TOWER COMPANIES

The largest wireless telecommunications carriers in the United States are currently AT&T, Verizon, T-Mobile, and Dish ("Boost Mobile"). These companies provide the network, the service, and the devices that individuals, companies, government agencies, and others use to communicate wirelessly.

These carriers are large publicly traded companies with market capitalizations ranging from $3 billion to $269 billion. T-Mobile is the largest at $269 billion. Dish, including Dish Wireless, is the smallest at just over $3 billion. Verizon and AT&T fall in at $178 billion and $170 billion, respectively. These numbers are current as of December 2024.

While the carriers themselves may be valued at billions of dollars, a significant percentage of their market value during the past few decades—aside from the carriers' end-user subscriptions—has been (and will likely continue to be) predicated on the ability of each carrier to expertly negotiate, renegotiate, leverage, execute, and extend the duration of a significant number of ground, tower, and rooftop leases. Similarly, network deployment and management are achieved through well-negotiated sale-leaseback agreements and MLAs ("Master License Agreements") with private and public tower companies and large corporate and government landlords. These negotiations, players, and objectives will likely remain the norm until improved or competing solutions in the market emerge.

In consideration of their market caps and access to capital, top carriers (and tower companies) are referred to as *investment-grade* tenants in the commercial real estate industry and usually earn ratings ranging from Lower Medium to High Grade by bond rating companies such as Standard & Poor's ("S&P"), Moody's, and Fitch. These investment-grade ratings increase the market value of cell tower leases where top carriers and public tower companies are named as ground, rooftop, or tower tenants. This rating also reduces the risk for lessors fortunate enough to have such high-quality national tenants. This risk reduction is relative to non-investment-grade lease tenants, which include small communications companies, small government agencies, local utilities, WISPs ("Wireless Internet Service Providers"), privately held companies, and private or individual tenants.

Lessors range from private individuals to government agencies, utilities to major corporations and non-profits, and everything in between. By leasing land from lessors, the tower companies and carriers provide lessors with increased financial security through regular and "dependable" payments, salable and exchangeable leases, and an opportunity to lease small spaces or vacant land to national investment-grade tenants. These opportunities rarely exist in real estate elsewhere or otherwise.

While carriers still own and develop cell towers, many carriers have sold a significant percentage of their cell tower portfolios to tower companies in conjunction with active leases or licenses. Since 2005, with Sprint leading the way, carriers began entering into various sale-leaseback agreements with tower companies. In these agreements, a tower company purchased a tower portfolio from a carrier and either leased or granted tower and ground space back to the carrier, or the tower company managed the tower portfolio while marketing the towers and available ground space on behalf of the carrier for a predetermined period.

By selling their towers or allowing tower companies to manage carrier-owned towers, the carriers were better positioned to finance, deploy, manage, and develop their respective networks (their core competency) in the near term. They could also reallocate resources away from real estate, which the tower companies were better suited to manage.

In contrast to carriers, large public tower companies operate as REITs ("Real Estate Investment Trusts"), allowing them to earn most of their revenue by leasing or purchasing the land on which towers will be constructed. They may also operate data centers, install and operate thousands of miles of fiber, and own and operate tens of thousands of small cells that work to supplement their existing macro cells. Finally, tower companies continue to partner with public, corporate, and private landlords to construct and manage towers and rooftops for carriers and other tenants on public and private property.

Like carriers, tower companies manage leases with property owners. Unlike carriers, tower companies often seek to acquire

their existing ground leases, most often in the form of an easement or a long-term prepayment, to stabilize asset equity, diminish long-term debt and risk, and ultimately increase profitability.
These lease buyouts appear to have been borne out of necessity
once third parties began purchasing ground leases directly from
property owners more than twenty years ago.

The top three U.S. tower company REITs—in terms of market cap
and tower count—are American Tower, Crown Castle, and SBA
Communications.

American Tower (NYSE: AMT)

American Tower (or "ATC" as industry insiders refer to it) is the
most valuable REIT in wireless telecom among the big three,
with a market cap of just over $92B (December 2024). ATC is
also the largest U.S. tower company. Its portfolio contains more
than 222,000 sites scattered throughout twenty-four countries:
Argentina, Australia, Bangladesh, Brazil, Burkina Faso, Canada,
Chile, Colombia, Costa Rica, France, Germany, Ghana, India,
Kenya, Mexico, Niger, Nigeria, Paraguay, Peru, Philippines,
Poland, South Africa, Spain, and Uganda. Among their holdings,
ATC counts more than 43,000 sites in the U.S. alone.

Crown Castle (NYSE: CCI)

As the number two tower company, CCI is the second-largest
REIT among the major U.S. tower companies. While Crown's
market cap was just over $60 billion in Q2 2023; since mid-
2023, Crown Castle has incurred three rounds of layoffs
(affecting more than 10% of its employees), and reducing its
market cap by more than 30% or $20 billion.

CCI is based in the U.S. and has over 40,000 domestic tower locations. Additionally, CCI has nearly 85,000 route miles of fiber optic and more than 100,000 small cells on air or under contract (although Crown — as of Q4 2024 — is selling its fiber business and reducing new small cell builds).

SBA Communications (NASDAQ(GS): SBAC)

SBA is another REIT. As of 2024, it owns or manages more than 33,000 towers, including more than 17,000 cell towers scattered throughout the United States (and its territories). As of December 2024, SBA had a market cap of about $23 billion.

CELL TOWER DEVELOPMENT

The type and existing use of potential cell tower properties is typically a secondary consideration to carriers and tower companies, assuming the site location, economics, access to utilities, access to a public road, soil, dimensions, and zoning suit their purposes. The need for cellular coverage in most areas requires carriers or tower companies to lease or purchase land in particular locations without much regard for a property's highest and best use.

Unlike typical real estate investment or development considerations, potential cell tower properties are not simply defined by variables such as views or simply "looking like a great place to put a cell tower." In my experience, many real estate brokers and investors assume otherwise.

Cell tower property locations are selected because they will address a coverage need in a given area of a cellular network, which is ultimately determined by using *Radio Frequency Engineering* (often referred to as an "RF Study"). RF studies determine (or confirm) a carrier's search ring, which is ultimately defined by the area, topography, population density, and the height at which a carrier seeks to construct a tower or install equipment atop an existing tower to fill an existing coverage gap. The carrier will use the method and location that achieves their requirements most quickly, efficiently, and cost-effectively.

It is usually much cheaper and easier for a carrier to install equipment on an existing tower (and is required by law in most instances). If the tower or the lease is not ideally suited for long-term tenancy, a carrier might seek to have a new tower built to avoid near-term future relocation, if possible.

When a carrier or tower company is looking for a new tower location, there may be several properties in an area that will meet the coverage requirements defined by the search ring. Still, the development and land lease/purchase costs vary greatly. Prospective lessors should never assume that, because they receive a call or letter proposing to construct a new cell tower on their property, other viable alternative sites do not exist.

Remember, carriers and tower companies will seek the least expensive solution to their problem like other businesses. That means if a lessor is seeking $2,500 per month and a neighbor will accept $1,500 per month, all other things being equal, the neighbor will likely get the deal.

In 2025, for example, it may cost $250,000 or more to build a monopole with a single tenant. If the ground rent becomes $2,500 per month instead of $1,500 per month, the cost of tenancy can increase by nearly $600,000 over 30 years (assuming a 3 percent annual escalator, with all options exercised). With that in mind, one can see the need for carriers and tower companies to carefully scrutinize their site selections.

LEASE AGGREGATORS

In the early 2000s—a few years after ATC and CCI emerged—
"lease aggregators" (or "aggregators") such as Unison and Wireless Capital Partners began to emerge in a meaningful way. As a
result, aggregators created a threat for carriers and tower companies alike. This forced carriers and tower companies to develop an answer to the rapid market changes they observed to
better protect their leasehold interests and infrastructure investments.

In response, most carriers and tower companies began incorporating a game changer into their leases known as the *Right of First
Refusal* ("*RoFR*"). Although RoFRs had existed throughout the U.S.
real estate industry for decades, in one form or another, the RoFR
is widely believed to have been incorporated into cell tower
leases as a direct result of, and as a deterrent to, lease aggregators
in the early 2000s.

The primary objective of the aggregator—much the same as any
lease investor—is to acquire cell tower lease rights in exchange
for a lump-sum cash buyout. Such a buyout is the advance payment of future lease cash flows in exchange for the assignment of
lease rights for a defined term and at a discounted price. This is
most often acquired with a recorded term or perpetual easement.
This process between the lessor and any lease investor is commonly referred to as lease monetization *(or capitalization)*.

Aggregators spend a great deal of time, effort, and money marketing to and contacting property owners on which cell towers
are constructed and for which there are active cell tower leases.
Aggregators focus on leases that do not contain a RoFR or those
with "weak" RoFRs.

Although some may view the aggregator segment of the wireless
industry with a critical eye, many would argue that aggregators
provide a much-needed funding alternative for lessors and real
estate investors alike. The presence of aggregators and private

investors has increased cell tower lease sale values and volumes. Otherwise, the cell tower lease market segment would have likely remained an oligopoly dominated by a few corporate giants, which would have suppressed competition, minimized alternatives, and held lease buyout values artificially lower.

TOWER PORTFOLIO AND LEASE BUYOUTS

Carriers and tower companies have long operated as if their individual and collective best interests would be much better served by buying out their leases or owning and managing them using exclusive agreements between carriers and tower companies. Yet, it still required a few years for carriers and tower companies to begin diligently pursuing solutions to this market threat beyond the RoFR.

This may also partially explain the logic behind the "tower company model," which began because of carrier portfolio sales to tower companies beginning in 2005 when Sprint sold approximately 6,600 towers to Global Signal (which later merged with Crown Castle) for the sum of $1.2 billion.

Similar multibillion-dollar transactions followed this event. The next occurred when T-Mobile sold 7,200 towers to Crown Castle for $2.4 billion in 2012. That was followed by AT&T's sale of 9,100 towers to Crown Castle in 2013 for $4.85 billion. Then, Verizon sold just over 11,300 towers to American Tower in 2015 for more than $5.06 billion.

Purchasing carrier assets generally made sense for tower companies in the long term (although carriers no longer appear to see it that way).

Tower companies also like to buy out their leases. When a tower company buys out its lease, such action will typically reduce its long-term holding cost and achieve an increased internal rate of return (IRR) on the asset purchased. Additional benefits for tower companies buying their leases include the ability to market excess capacity on existing towers for a longer duration, a reduction in (or complete elimination of) previously required lessor approvals, and the reduction or elimination of the threat of ground lease termination at lease expiration.

LEASE OPTIMIZERS

As an additional response to aggregators, carriers and tower companies also developed relationships with firms such as The Lyle Company, Md7, Tower Alliance, or Black Dot (called "lease optimizers" or "optimizers"). This was done to reach out to lessors to renegotiate or extend cell tower leases (known as "lease optimizations" or "optimizations"). It also increased lease buyouts to reduce the number of leases sold to unaffiliated third parties.

Such optimizations are the least expensive and least risky means by which carriers and tower companies achieve the greatest amount of control over their infrastructure and lease assets for an extended period. The optimizations also create an opportunity for the optimization company—on behalf of their tower company or carrier clients—to attempt to incorporate a RoFR, a Non-Compete, and other undesirable clauses into the lease terms (which will most often be detrimental to the landowner) if one or more is not already in place.

When an optimizer contacts a lessor, it is often to discuss a lease extension, amendment, or rent guarantee offer. The rent guarantee will guarantee lease payments for a period and further "guarantee" that the lease will not be terminated in exchange for the lessor agreeing to a monthly or periodic lease rate reduction and/or an annual or periodic escalator.

Alternatively, optimization companies sometimes approach a lessor with a choice wherein the lessor will be pressured to accept a reduction in lease rate and/or escalator or face "immediate" lease cancelation/site decommissioning.

While this argument appears plausible in a small percentage of cell tower leases, lessors are advised to hire a qualified lease consultant to determine the likelihood of lease cancelation without agreeing to a "proposed" rent and/or escalator reduction.

One should also know that optimizers often send a letter using a lessee's letterhead or an email from a lessee's email address, even though an optimizer works as a third party for the lessee. In these letters, optimizers imply that time is of the essence. They do this by providing short "respond by" dates with a string of premises or rationale by which the request is being proffered.

It's also worth noting that optimizers may approach a lessor by saying something like, "We have analyzed your site on behalf of our client XYZ Corp, and the lease—at $3,XXX per month—is about $1,XXX more than the lease rate for five of our closest sites." If they do not offer any data on the closest sites, please ask for it. After receiving that data, any dialogue should start with the following questions:

- Does your client own the tower in question? If not, who does?

- What are the locations of the other towers you referenced?

- How much was the starting rent for the other towers you referenced?

- Does your client *own* any of the other towers?

- Are there collocates on the tower at the site in question?

- Are there any carrier applications pending at the site in question?

- How many tenants are on each of the other towers?

- How tall are the other towers?

- Can you share the contact information of the other lessor?

- How old are the leases on the other sites?

- How much are the other lease escalators?

- How big are the other compound areas?

- How many amendments have occurred on each of the other site leases?

- Are the other sites hardened or ungraded to 5G? Is the site in question hardened or upgraded to 5G?

- What is the zoning for the other sites?

This kind of response usually garners a lengthy pause followed by, "I'll have to call you back."

Now, you haven't said "no" to anything; all you've done is request more details. If the threat is real, the optimizer will continue to contact you and attempt to provide answers to your questions.

One final point about optimizers: Optimization firm representatives are paid based on the savings they deliver to their clients.

Period. So, while there are always potential risks when a lessor is contacted about reductions, cancelations, guarantees, etc., the fact that such a proposal comes from an optimizer should be an indication that the optimizer is examining the site based only on the rent being paid relative to the rest of the local market or some predetermined rent cap. As you likely understand by now, that may not be what it appears to be.

That said, although the cancelation of any cell tower lease can occur for various reasons, the reasons for a lease termination are likely to be obvious and are only considered by carriers or tower companies as a last resort or when strategically imperative.

For example, when the T-Mobile-Sprint merger was finalized, it was well-known that upward of 35,000 (primarily Sprint sites) were going on the chopping block, as 10,000 or so new T-Mobile sites were coming online. As it turns out, various Sprint *and* T-Mobile sites have been decommissioned. The superior lease likely prevailed if there were redundant sites—particularly on the same tower. That would ultimately remove the equipment associated with the inferior lease and relocate equipment as required.

Despite the reputation some people seem to imply about optimizers (or perhaps just the companies), the optimizers with whom I have spoken have always been professional and polite.

END OF THE TOWER COMPANY MODEL?

A few years after selling off tens of thousands of their assets to the tower companies, AT&T and Verizon are now saying: "The tower company model is unsustainable." In 2016, for example, AT&T openly solicited bids from real estate developers to build new towers close to existing cellular locations to give the carriers negotiating leverage.

In November 2017, AT&T and Verizon entered a joint venture with Tillman Infrastructure to collocate on hundreds of new Tillman build-to-suit towers near an existing tower where both carriers were currently tenants, with the possibility of many more collocations in the future. Each carrier has since allegedly reduced the number of new tower builds with ATC, CCI, and SBA. They are apparently seeking to build many more with the likes of Tillman and various other smaller tower companies.

The benefit to this strategy is twofold: 1) Lower tower build costs, and 2) The payment terms and escalators are (per Tillman) "more conducive to a long-term carrier relationship." In other words, it is a better value for carriers.

As it turned out, the tower company model was great for the carriers when they unloaded a management headache and picked up billions of dollars by selling their respective tower portfolios to the tower companies. However, those leases have escalated significantly since the large asset sales and relative to the lease rates of just a decade ago.

While each of the carriers still appears to be actively pursuing rent reductions or optimizations in one form or another, it will take some time for the carriers to reduce their reliance on CCI, ATC, or SBA—if that ever occurs—while also meeting their respective network management and deployment objectives.

PRIVATE TOWER COMPANIES: A CARRIER ALTERNATIVE TO THE BIG THREE?

In addition to American Tower, Crown Castle, and SBA Communications, several private tower companies ("PTCs") have emerged during the past few years. Many of these began life as aggregators. They continue to operate similarly, except that they are now *also* building and buying towers and are now in direct competition with the big three tower companies.

TowerPoint, Everest Infrastructure Partners, Symphony Wireless, Peppertree ("K2"), and Diamond Communications have made a name for themselves in the wireless telecom industry. Please understand that PTCs often have access to hundreds of millions or billions of dollars in capital. This has become true over the years, or decades, of strong track records, during which time each has proven capable of purchasing and managing wireless assets individually and in portfolios.

As an example of PTC potential, in June 2021, Diamond Communications, LLC ("Diamond") purchased Melody Wireless Infrastructure, Inc. ("MWI") for the sum of $1.625 billion. The sale included MWI's portfolio of 2,300 tenanted wireless communications sites. It was one of the largest PTC purchases in history and may foreshadow what's to come. According to Ed Farscht, Diamond's CEO, the purchase "...will solidify Diamond's position as one of the largest privately held wireless infrastructure companies in the United States."

Considering the above account and examining what's occurring in the cell tower industry today, it isn't difficult to fathom a distinct market shift wherein a group of investors (or PTCs) make a big push for at-risk tower company assets. Based on reported domestic ground lease extension and acquisition numbers during the past few years—as published in public tower company periodic filings and as demonstrated on the ground—it shouldn't be a monumental task, nor a surprise to anyone.

CHAPTER 4
WIRELESS INFRASTRUCTURE AS WELL AS EXISTING & EMERGING WIRELESS TECHNOLOGIES

W hile one doesn't need to become an expert on wireless infrastructure to be an effective cell tower landlord, I believe one should understand the basics of the industry's most common infrastructure and technology types. It will lead to a better understanding of cell towers, industry, and site-specific changes. It will also better prepare one to capitalize on opportunities that others will miss when negotiating with those in the industry. With that in mind, this chapter will provide an overview of wireless infrastructure technologies.

For links to important websites in the wireless industry, please refer to Appendix A at the back of the book. For pictures of the various technologies and infrastructure types, refer to Appendix B.

WIRELESS INFRASTRUCTURE

The U.S.'s most well-known and discussed wireless infrastructure categories can be grouped into eleven general categories.

Macro Cells

Macro cells (macro cell towers) refer to monopoles, lattice, and guyed towers. The category also includes monopines, mono-palms, rooftop installations, water tower installations, church steeples, flagpoles, clock towers, and more. These are used in urban, suburban, and rural markets, serving as the transmission hub of cellular networks. Each type of cell tower serves a different purpose and requires a different property size. Heights typically range from 50 feet to 300 feet or more.

Super Cells

Super cells are similar to macro cells but larger. They can rise as high as 2,000 feet and serve in place of up to 25 macro cells. They save cell tower companies and carriers in development costs associated with building cell towers. Under the right conditions, super cells can cover more than sixty times the area a typical 100-foot monopole covers. Super cells can also be constructed using existing guyed towers from the broadcast industry, fitted with high-gain, narrow-sectored antenna to increase range and capacity.

Distributed Antenna Systems ("DAS")

A distributed antenna system is called a network of antenna that sends and receives cellular signals on a carrier's licensed frequencies. A DAS improves voice and data connectivity for end users and can be designed to suit various applications. DAS comprises iDAS (for indoor applications) and oDAS (for outdoor applications). Other applications include eDAS, active DAS, passive DAS, hybrid DAS, and off-air DAS.

For instance, DAS networks provide wireless network coverage in large shopping malls, sports stadiums, conference centers, corporate campuses, hotels, and almost anywhere macro cells may have difficulty reaching or suffer signal degradation due to building construction, maximum facility capacity, or some combination of both.

DAS distributes the signal but does not generate the signal itself. The signal comes from small cells, a base station, a roof antenna, or a combination of one or more technologies. Upon receipt of the signal, the DAS will distribute the signal through the facility in which it is installed. Such distribution is accomplished using one of the four currently available: digital, passive, hybrid, and active.

The type of DAS network designed and installed in a facility depends on several variables that may include:

- Exterior signal strength provided by an adjacent tower or towers

- Facility construction materials

- Height and size of the facility

- Number of users inside the building at peak capacity

- Number of carriers required

- Scalability

- Access to high-speed Internet (fiber)

- Performance requirements

- Budget

As of 2024, DAS is one of the main technology types deployed in large commercial and enterprise facility applications throughout the U.S.

CBRS (discussed below) purports to offer a cost-effective alternative to DAS architecture soon.

Small Cells

Small cells include pico cells, micro cells, and femtocells. They are a series of low-powered antenna that work along the edges of and in conjunction with macro cells. These cells provide increased coverage in previously hard-to-reach areas and increased capacity through expanded wireless density. Small cells are primarily constructed outside using streetlights, utility poles, slim line poles, and other city street infrastructure, including bus enclosures, statues, billboards, and other outside displays.

Today, while most small cell infrastructure deployments are targeted for outdoor use, indoor small cell systems are also used in some applications and may or may not incorporate Wi-Fi or unlicensed LTE bands ("LTE-U")/Licensed Assisted Access ("LAA"), depending on the capabilities that service providers choose to support.

Groups of small cells or DAS work in conjunction with macro cells and comprise a *heterogeneous network* ("*HetNet*"); a network agreement or license often governs such developments.

Wi-Fi

Wi-Fi is a catch-all term defined as wireless networking technology used to interface with the Internet. Some claim that Wi-Fi started in the Hawaiian Islands in 1971 under the name of "AlohaNet" and was used to connect the islands.

Beyond that, the history of Wi-Fi gets murky. Various individuals, entities, and organizations claim to be a part of Wi-Fi's prodigious past. As it is known today, Wi-Fi was originally launched for widespread consumer use in 1999.

Throughout the twenty-plus years of serious and continuous development of Wi-Fi since its rollout in 1999, there have been numerous increases in speed and capacity, ever-increasing range, and security (which was conspicuously absent in early versions of Wi-Fi). During that time, Wi-Fi has spanned six generations, all of which are IEEE Standard 802.11, with the current version known as "Wi-Fi 6E."

Wi-Fi 6E (not to be confused with Wi-Fi 6) was first introduced in 2021 under the IEEE Standard 802.11ax. It provides 3x greater wireless connection speeds than Wi-Fi 5, with peak speeds of 9.6 Gbps and a significant reduction in latency. It is considered the biggest Wi-Fi advancement for consumers in the past twenty years.

The newest version of Wi-Fi is known as Wi-Fi 7. Expected to be released in 2024, it will feature the IEEE Standard 802.11be and may reach up to 40 Gbps.

In addition to allowing consumers to connect to the Internet wirelessly, one of the greatest advancements to date (which can be attributed to Wi-Fi) was the advent of Wi-Fi calling in 2007. Wi-Fi calling permitted cell phone users to make and receive calls in locations where carrier service was spotty (which was very common in those days). It also reduced carrier network conges-tion and costs to the consumer by reducing the use of carrier data.

Citizens Broadband Radio Services ("CBRS")

The Federal Communications Commission (FCC) defines Citizens Broadband Radio Services as "a private, two-way, short-distance voice communications service for personal or business activities of the general public." It is a mix of licensed and "lightly licensed" services depending on a user's tier (there are three tiers). It also may be used for voice paging.

CBRS uses forty channels, and its purpose is to provide more spectrum for mobile use and to make private LTE network devel-opment possible while expanding 4G and 5G services. The net ef-fect will create cheaper, more reliable, and more available wire-less services.

There will likely be many applications in which CBRS will replace Wi-Fi, especially when a longer range is required or when forms of signal interference can disrupt unlicensed Wi-Fi.

Fiber Optic ("Fiber" or "Optical Fiber")

A fiber optic cable consists of up to a few hundred optical (glass) fibers bundled together into a cable. Fiber provides four primary benefits:

1. Increased speed and capacity over alternatives such as copper and DSL

2. Delivers very high-speed Internet

3. Less speed loss over long distances and immunity to electromagnetic interference relative to copper wiring

4. Sets a new speed standard for fixed and wireless Internet in the U.S.

Fiber transmits data in the form of light using a process known as *total internal reflection*. Despite rumors of the contrary, the speed at which light travels through fiber optic cable is about 31 percent slower than the speed of light.

Fiber optics also employs repeaters at periodic intervals to regenerate the optical signal by converting it to an electric signal, processing that newly created electrical signal, and then retransmitting the fiber optic signal.

Currently, most fiber providers offer speeds up to 1 Gbps, but a few commercial providers offer speeds reported to be up to 10 Gbps.

Fiber can be broken into two basic categories: single-mode and multi-mode. Single-mode is typically used for long-distance applications; single-mode fiber also enjoys a much higher bandwidth than multi-mode. Single-mode is also less expensive than multi-mode fiber.

Multi-mode fiber is designed to span shorter distances. Multi-mode uses a larger diameter cable than single-mode, which permits more than one light pulse to travel through the cable simultaneously, thereby increasing the data capacity relative to single-mode fiber. Multi-mode is also more prone to signal loss and interference than its single-mode counterpart.

Finally, where single-mode fiber typically uses a laser as its light source, multi-mode fiber generally uses an LED.

Backhaul

Backhaul transmits voice, data, and video between a cell tower and a mobile switching center (MSC) or alternative to a fixed or wireless network.

Most network operators employ a combination of fixed and wireless backhaul infrastructure to connect their networks (and customers) to the Internet, with wireless backhaul being more ideal and cost-effective for shorter distances. In contrast, fixed backhaul is better suited to long distances.

Initially, as with all wireless segments, carrier backhaul speeds were slow, using T1 lines, then T3 lines (equal to 28 T1 lines) for their connection to the Internet.

Next came higher-speed 3G HSPA+, which replaced T1 and T3 backhaul until the advent of Ethernet, which brought speeds of 100Mbps.

Finally, with the development of 4G LTE, carrier backhaul speeds increased to 1Gbps+, which was the chosen backhaul tech in most parts of the U.S. until recently. With the advent of 5G, several competing backhaul technologies exist, each providing exponentially greater speed than 4G LTE backhaul technology.

Unfortunately, there are limitations associated with using fiber as part of a backhaul solution, including installation difficulties and cost. Also, while carriers have used microwave backhaul for remote areas, the connection speeds for microwave backhaul are lower than fixed alternatives, there are capacity and climate issues, and applications are usually limited to line-of-sight. Recently, in response to the need for a cost-effective, reliable broadband solution for rural areas, WISPs were also developed.

Fronthaul

Fronthaul refers to the transmission of voice, data, and video using dark fiber—also referred to as "Fiber to the Small Cell" ("FTTS")—between a cell tower's centralized baseband unit ("BBU") to a small cell, which is sometimes referred to as a remote radio head ("RRH"). The small cell fronthaul is connected to a mobile switching center ("MSC") on the carrier's backhaul network.

In theory, fronthaul allows wireless carriers to reduce the required macro cells, which ostensibly saves both CapEx and OpEx. That said, carriers are now questioning the overall savings versus historical projections because of the number of small cells required to complement each macro cell.

Wireless Internet Service Provider ("WISP")

Wireless Internet Service Providers provide cost-effective, high-speed Internet to rural customers. They operate in all fifty states, with services provided by more than 2,800 providers. WISPs currently serve more than 7 million customers with typical download speeds between 25 Mbps and 100 Mbps for residential applications and up to 1 Gbps for business applications.

Data Centers

Data centers can be mobile, virtual, or stationary (permanent) and are defined as highly secure locations (with multiple security, temperature, humidity, and fire protection systems in place). They are often housed in a well-constructed or high-rise (Class A) building with multi-redundant and instantaneous power backups. These might include diesel generators, batteries, and redundant substations, which are high-quality, stable, and uninterrupted power supplies located near urban or suburban areas. These locations allow for storing and processing large amounts of proprietary or highly sensitive data using computers, networks, servers, and other sensitive processing and transmission equipment necessary for high-volume business operations in real time. Data centers can support the most advanced current and emerging technologies.

WIRELESS TECHNOLOGIES

Since the advent of wireless technology, wireless communications have developed through several generations of improvements. Let's look at some of the latest developments.

5G: Definition and Performance Metrics

5G refers to the Fifth Generation of wireless technology. It includes the integration of devices (otherwise known as the Internet of Things ("IoT")) that allow us to become increasingly connected to the Internet in a much more meaningful and useful way than we have experienced in years past. Such devices include wearable tech, household management, health care and monitoring, connected family members, etc.

The main drivers of 5G are five-fold:

1. Increased bandwidth

2. Increased speed

3. Reduced latency

4. Enhanced capacity

5. Network densification

Combining these will deliver the benefits of expansive Artificial Intelligence and Virtual Reality. While 5G is just a step in our collective technological walk, it's rapidly becoming the biggest and most transformative step yet. For example, a two-hour video now requires just a few seconds to download on 5G versus a few minutes to download the same movie using 4G.

As of 2024, the following 5G standards should be fulfilled in the U.S.:

- Download speeds increased by 100+x vs. 4G LTE

- Latency reduced by 99 percent vs. 4G LTE

- Spectral efficiency enhanced 20-25x compared to 4G LTE

- Coverage is expected to reach 45 percent of the world's population

- 5G will support 600x the number of devices of 4G per square mile

Millimeter Wave ("mmWave") was to be a game changer as a part of 5G. Concerning speed, mmWave delivers, but it cannot penetrate glass or trees (or a number of other manmade or natural hindrances), and the tech still provides a very small fraction of network time to the average mobile user. U.S. carriers have largely moved away from mmWave in favor of the mid-band spectrum, as while mid-band does not offer the speed of mmWave, it is still quite fast and provides better coverage.

As of this writing, only about 25 countries have licensed mmWave, and with the additional costs phone manufacturers incur—and pass on to consumers—to incorporate mmWave into phones, it does not yet appear that widespread adoption of mmWave has yet occurred or is on the horizon (at least as of 2024).

Health Concerns Surrounding 5G

While the benefits of 5G technology are undeniable, one must also consider the potential health risks its advancements may deliver in the process. According to a paper published by Martin L. Pall, PhD, of Washington State University, several studies have been conducted that provide scientific certainty for each of eight pathophysiological effects caused by non-thermal microwave frequency EMF exposure. A copy of the study can be found at https://ehtrust.org/wp-content/uploads/5g-emf-hazards-dr-martin-l.-pall-eu-emf2018-6-11us3.pdf.

This is not to say that claims of adverse health consequences associated with earlier generations of wireless technologies were never made. Even so, such concerns have grown among some individuals since 5G was first introduced.

I'm not taking a position on the information published by Dr. Pall or similar publications about the purported health consequences of 5G. Still, I feel it is an issue that the reader should be aware of as it provides a more comprehensive view of the industry, where it has taken us, and where we might go as a consequence.

5.5 G

5.5G is expected to be commercialized sometime in 2024, with claims of up to a 10x increase in network speeds (from 5G) and new IoT and sensing capabilities.

Beyond that, 5.5G is expected to act as an upgraded version of 5G, with 10 Gbps downlink, 100 billion connections, endogenous intelligence, and expanded capabilities. It will act as a bridge between 5G and 6G and deliver widespread autonomous vehicle capability, an enhanced Internet of Things, increased robotics and manufacturing capabilities, and advances in medical and other current and emerging industry sectors.

6G

While work on the Sixth Generation of wireless technology is on the way, the first commercial networks aren't expected until, at the earliest, 2028.

How will 6G be different from 5G?

6G will use more advanced radio equipment and a greater volume and diversity of airwaves than 5G. That includes using the Extreme High Frequency (EHF) spectrum, delivering ultra-high speeds and huge capacity over short distances.

What will 6G be able to do?

Faster speeds, greater capacity, and lower latency will free emerging applications from the constraints of local processing power, connect more devices to the network, and blur the lines between the physical man and digital worlds. Existing services will be transformed, and 6G could be the network enhancement that finally delivers services previously observed only in science fiction.

How will 6G change or improve on 5G?

6G will pick up where 5G & 5.5G leave off, initially offering high data throughputs of 100+ Gbps with the extra low latency required for advanced applications, including enhanced artificial intelligence and real-time virtual reality to improve the human experience.

Key drivers for 6G include ultra-high-speed connectivity to rural areas, intelligent monitoring to improve energy and transportation efficiencies, immersive remote presence, digital twins, holographic telepresence, and extended reality.

When will 6G happen?

Recent industry predictions indicate that the development of 6G has already begun, and standards and early commercial availability will likely be completed around 2028. If that timeline holds, we should see the first 6G products around that time. Widespread deployment won't likely occur until 2030 or beyond.

CTIA: THE INDUSTRY BY THE NUMBERS

According to the 2022 CTIA Annual Survey (which you can find at https://api.ctia.org/wp-content/uploads/2022/09/Summary-of-CTIAs-Wireless-Industry-Survey-2022.pdf), it is estimated that there were more than 419,000 active cell sites in the U.S. by Q1 2022. That number includes an estimated 67,871 new cell sites activated between 2018 and 2020. That represents a greater than 35 percent increase in the number of new sites since 2016 and shows that more new cell sites were built between 2018 and 2021 than were built in the previous seven years combined.

As of 2023, carriers and tower companies still appear to be building new towers at a rate faster than tower companies (and third-party buyers combined) can acquire existing towers and leases. Based on the CTIA report and CapEx projections from carriers and tower companies for the next few years, it appears that new tower growth will continue to outpace tower and lease acquisitions for the foreseeable future.

STARLINK

With the recent advent of StarLink—an LEO satellite "constellation" orbiting the Earth—access to high-speed, low-latency, high-capacity wireless broadband is now a reality in many parts of the world. Starlink (StarLink.com) currently provides residential, business, maritime, roaming, and aviation solutions. Starlink's specifications claim at least 99 percent availability in current service locations with 25-50 ms latency, 20-220 Mbps (download), and 5-25 Mbps (upload) for fixed service plans. Their specifications for mobile service plans currently claim <99 ms latency, 5-250 Mbps (download), and 2-30 Mbps (upload). The above figures are current as of December 2024, and speeds vary depending on the plan chosen.

CHAPTER 5
CELL TOWER LEASES, CELL TOWER LEASE SALES, AND WIDELY USED CELL TOWER LEASE CLAUSES AND TERMS

I first came across a cell tower lease in the late 1990s. I wasn't impressed or entirely understood what lurked beneath the benign surface—even in the '90s.

While nothing jumped out at me initially, I quickly began to identify some of the subtleties used by industry leaders to capitalize on the disparity in understanding between carriers and most landlords.

In this chapter, I'll cover the basics of cell tower leases, including defining and explaining typical terms. I'll also outline lease extensions, amendments, successor leases, and clauses to look out for.

CELL TOWER LEASES

Some original, simpler cell tower leases still active today remain much the same as when drafted some thirty years ago. Many have continued without additional lease conditions and may remain within the original option terms.

Unfortunately, for many landlords, the cell tower leases drafted or amended during the past twenty years have become increasingly complex and restrictive relative to their predecessors. The market has experienced expansion and consolidation, contains more sites, and has become more efficient and experienced. The result is enhanced competition and much more technical negotiation considerations (which can be problematic for the under-informed landlord).

49

PARTIES TO CELL TOWER LEASES

Like any commercial lease, cell tower leases involve at least two parties. The first party is the "Lessor," which may also be the landlord, the property owner, or the property manager. Additionally, there is the "Lessee," who could also be referred to as the tenant, the carrier, or the tower company.

TYPES OF CELL TOWER AGREEMENTS

Most wireless telecommunications agreements are called "cell tower leases" or "cell tower licenses," "ground leases" or "ground licenses," "rooftop antenna leases" or "rooftop antenna licenses," "network agreements," and "master license agreements."

Throughout the rest of Cell Tower Secrets, the phrases "cell tower lease," "ground lease," "tower lease," "rooftop license," "license," or "lease" may be used interchangeably when describing or discussing all lease and license types, installations, or applications, unless otherwise specified.

A cell tower lease is the primary legal instrument by which tower companies and carriers define the terms under which they will lease land and/or tower space from a lessor. In the cell tower industry, leases of this variety may be referred to as "ground leases," while leases of the tower space may be referred to as "tower leases"; in some cases, both ground and tower leases are covered by a single lease.

A cell tower or rooftop/structure antenna, along with the transmission equipment and backhaul installed at a given location, is called a "cell site." Cell sites may include more than one wireless tenant and be governed by one or multiple leases or licenses.

Tower or structure leases for sub-tenants may also be subject to a separate ground lease between the sub-tenant and the lessor unless the primary tenant has ground lease rights to sub-lease ground space and the available space to do so.

In contrast to ground leases, the leases that occur between tower companies and carriers, or carriers and other carriers, are referred to in the industry as "antenna site agreements," "site lease agreements," or "license agreements" (often in the form of an MLA, which may be used between parties across many properties or sites). Agreements of this nature are used to allocate leasehold interest on a cell tower and/or ground space between the primary tenant (also referred to as the lessee) and the sub-tenant (also referred to as the sub-lessee).

THE DIFFERENCE BETWEEN A LICENSE AND A LEASE

A cell tower or ground *license*, in contrast to a cell tower or ground *lease*, is used when the licensor grants permission to a licensee to conduct an action on the owner's property. The primary difference is that a lease gives an individual or entity the right to <u>control the property.</u> In contrast, a license only gives an individual or entity <u>the right to act on the property</u>.

CELL TOWER LEASE SALES ("MONETIZATION")

The following is a simplified explanation of how the industry functions and how lease sales are funded.

Most cell tower lease investors are tower companies, lease aggregators, or private investors. Depending on the lease investor type, the structure of a given lease acquisition is likely very different. After all, different organizations and individuals will have different motivations, requirements, and qualifications. They will likely have dissimilar tax considerations and diverging short-term and long-term objectives.

When lease aggregators or private tower companies require capital, they seek the lowest-cost capital they can obtain (typically in some version of a debt and equity stack), mostly from private or public sources such as family offices, private investors, insurance companies, or investment banks.

Aggregators, or private tower companies, then use the capital to purchase the rights to current and successor leases, which will be held in an investment vehicle (often an LLC). The LLCs may be used to purchase hundreds or thousands of sites, often worth hundreds of millions or more by the time the portfolio is finally sold.

In most instances, the capital received at the sale will be used to pay off the debt, and the seller will begin building another portfolio using a new entity and round of funding. Alternatively, smaller private investors often retain leases for the margins earned from them, assuming that the objective yield will be met by doing so. They also do this to bank on future lease renegotiation potential.

Although the answer to what ultimately happens with each cell tower lease upon monetization may be somewhat different, the net result to the lessor is very much the same: the sale of future lease cash flows in exchange for a discounted lump-sum payment or payments in advance of the payment schedule, with some variation as to precisely which lease rights are being sold and for what duration. Another difference, of course, will likely be the price.

It's also worth noting that some legitimate reasons exist for lessors to sell their leases. I am often asked, "Why should I sell, and why does anyone want to buy my lease?"

In some cases, the answer is the decommission risk. In most cases, however, it simply boils down to comparing the long-term cash flow value of the lease (when considering extensions, possible amendments, inflation, lease escalators, and current rents vs.

ongoing decommission risks) relative to the current lease sale value.

Perhaps even more significant is that many of the largest lease buyers hold hundreds or thousands of these assets. Because of this, they have increased negotiating leverage while being able to spread risk across many assets. That is not usually the case for small- or medium-sized lessors.

TYPES OF LEASE SALES AND METHODS OF PAYMENT

The sale of cell tower lease cash flows can take a variety of forms defined by several different industry names—short-term lease purchase, long-term lease purchase, perpetual easement, term easement, pre-paid lease, purchase of lease and successor lease rights, assignment of lease—and the type and duration of the lease rights sold may also determine the structure of the lease buyout, typically either installment or lump-sum.

The difference in the cell tower lease purchase form can determine the amount of money the lessor will receive because of the sale and will dictate which rights are retained by the lessor versus those assigned to or inherited by the lease purchaser. It can also determine the duration of future payments sold, which typically ranges from ten years to perpetuity.

CELL TOWER LEASE STRUCTURES AND IMPORTANT LEASE TERMS

Cell tower leases are often structured like triple net ("NNN") commercial real estate leases and will typically be drafted with one or two 6- to 12-month option periods followed by an initial 5- to 10-year lease term. After that, multiple 5-year option terms, potentially extending the lease to a total duration of twenty to fifty years or more, is the industry norm.

JAMES KENNEDY

During the cell tower lease duration, lessees will often approach the lessor to discuss the execution of a lease amendment, lease extension, or successor lease. I'll discuss all of these in more detail later in this chapter.

Additionally, most of these leases contain an early termination provision designed to permit the lessee to terminate the lease with as little as a 30- to 90-day notice, for any one of many acceptable reasons or no reason at all, and with virtually zero penalties. Although the possibility of tower or lease decommissioning always exists, it is not the norm.

It is also important to note that although a cell tower lease may often appear to mimic a NNN commercial lease, several other considerations and tenant objectives can cause the cell tower lease to affect the property and lessor in ways not contemplated by the traditional commercial or residential real estate lease. Such considerations are caused by the fact that tower or ground leases are proprietary and are often one-sided in favor of the lessee. Additional considerations and objectives will be discussed throughout the book (in various contexts).

CELL TOWER LEASE STRUCTURE AND CONTENT OVERVIEW

Before purchasing or selling a cell tower lease, with or without real estate, it is important that you take some time to familiarize yourself with the standard clauses contained in a cell tower lease. The following section will explain the standard lease clauses and the contents of possible extensions and amendments. Afterward, you'll better understand the intent of each of these and the effect they can have on the lease and underlying real estate.

Most cell tower leases are structured similarly, even though companies use different attorneys to draft lease documents. Also, considerations vary by site, laws vary from state to state, and leases can certainly change over time. That said, except for a few standout clauses (such as the RoFR), the basic elements of cell tower leases have remained much the same for decades. The result and the value of a given lease will also have much to do with the original lease negotiation.

Cell tower leases contain many sections that define every nuance of the relationship between the lessor and lessee. The following list represents the clauses that may be included in a cell tower lease. While those listed may not be present in every lease, they are in cell tower leases and often appear in this order (or in an order close to this layout).

Lease Title or Property Name/ID – A name or property ID is at the top or bottom of almost every lease. The property address may be included, as well.

Parties – This section lists the lessor, the lessee, and each party's mailing address. It may also include the effective or commencement date of the transaction.

Property – This section of the cell tower lease will often include the APN (assessor's parcel number or other parcel ID) along with reference to Exhibit "A," which may include the premises, leased areas, legal descriptions, and a site survey. The "Property" is the parcel (or parcels) of land on which the Premises is located.

Premises – This section defines the area of the lease compound, easements, the equipment, the tower, and the tower's location on the Property. The Premises are usually fenced or otherwise separate from the remainder of the property. Premises are generally not the same as Property.

Permitted Use or Use – This section outlines the proposed and permitted use of the leased area(s) and the requirements, limitations, and restrictions of such use. It also outlines each party's responsibilities in obtaining the necessary approvals for such use of the premises. This may include, but isn't limited to:

- Which party to the lease will be responsible for the costs associated with installing and maintaining equipment and improvements? Sometimes, each party participates in the costs or responsibilities of any installation or management.

- The types of improvements and equipment to be installed, often also including dimensions, descriptions, and limits of each.

- Lessee's rights to access, fencing, hours of operation, equipment repairs, equipment replacement/upgrades or changes, material alterations, modifications, permitted frequencies, expansions, and other activities required to operate the site unless specifically conditioned or prohibited.

It's important to clearly define the "permitted use" or "use," as failure to do so may provide the lessee with unexpected rights in response to market changes or lessee needs. It may also cause other undesirable implications or consequences due to ambiguity.

Conditions Precedent – The conditions set forth by the lessee that must occur for the lease to become (or remain) binding. If conditions or precedents are not met, the lessee usually reserves the right to terminate the lease without further obligation or liability to the lessor.

Term – Outlines the definition of the initial lease term, the start date or event of the initial lease term (often referred to as the "Commencement Date"), the lessee's option to extend (often referred to as "Renewal Term"), and conditions of the lessee's renewal rights. Be certain to pay attention to terms that may appear similar but often cause confusion, such as Effective Date, Execution Date, and Commencement Date, as they likely have somewhat different meanings that can make a sizable difference on the front end of a lease.

Rent – Outlines the initial and regular rent during the lease, the date on which the rent will be due throughout the lease, and any rent increases throughout the initial and subsequent lease terms. When negotiating a new lease, a lease extension, or a lease amendment (including a rent increase), it is important to seek payments or increases in payments as quickly as possible. Otherwise, most carriers and tower companies will use your property for months with no compensation or without the negotiated compensation increase in effect. In some instances, at the time of negotiation for a lease amendment or extension, retroactive payment increases are warranted and will be approved.

Installation – This section outlines the lessee's acceptable delivery, construction, and installation methods. That includes:

- Any facade or cosmetic upgrades;

- Fencing, landscaping, and hardscape;

- A tower or antennas;

- Fiber optic lines (or other means of backhaul), and

- Any electric, gas, or water lines.

The Installation section should clearly define all the terms of installation, and it should include the duration of construction, the use of a crane, trenching, permits, bonds, insurance, operating in the right-of-way, hours, debris control, delays, and anything else that would normally be considered in conjunction with construction.

Improvements, Access – Outlines the lessee's rights concerning access, construction, installation of equipment and fencing, installation of transmission and utility lines, title to lessee's facilities and equipment, equipment removal, utilities, lease termination, and so on.

Interference with Communications – This section outlines how broadcast equipment will be operated on the premises. It also covers the rights and remedies of the lessee regarding any interference that may occur on the premises, whether the lessor or lessee causes such interference.

Non-Compete – Non-compete clauses are used by carriers and tower companies to prevent a lessor from leasing ground space in the future to competing carriers or tower companies on the same—or adjacent—property on which an initial tower or rooftop antenna has been constructed. The problem is that some form of a non-compete clause may be slipped into a lease or amendment unnoticed (and may appear rather benign). The net effect to the lessor is that the existing wireless lease tenant may gain control over the entire property—relative to wireless infrastructure—for the entire lease term (including option periods). If that happens, any additional carrier or tower company will be permitted to build infrastructure (i.e., a cell tower or rooftop antenna) only with the permission of the original tenant and often with little or no additional revenue to the lessor! **PLEASE BE CAREFUL WITH THIS ONE!**

Personal or Property Taxes – Outlines the premises' breakdown and payment terms for personal and property taxes. These are often allocated as real property taxes for the land and personal property taxes for improvements, including the tower, broadcast equipment, fences, and most other structures or accessories.

The terms here are typically structured as a proportionate share of the ground area plus fixtures payable by the lessee for any verifiable tax increase attributable to the lessee's equipment. In any case, one should verify if the lessee has or will obtain a separate property tax account or if the lessee will need to be billed for any reimbursements.

If the lessee has its own tax account, there is likely little to worry about. Otherwise, the property tax bill(s) should be checked (at least) annually if the property tax account is entirely in the lessor's name. Any property taxes due by the lessee will likely require the lessor to bill the lessee for any reimbursements. Such billings may be subject to appeal by the lessee before any reimbursement to the lessor is paid.

Termination – Outlines the conditions and terms by which either party may terminate the lease. As in most ground leases, the lessee often has the option to terminate the lease with short notice—as little as 30 to 90 days—for any reason or no reason. The same is not usually true for the lessor. It is worth noting that the termination clause can be renegotiated during the lease life cycle and may become biased toward the lessor as a lease approaches expiration, is extended, or otherwise amended.

Notice Address – Effective communication between the parties is important. Therefore, each party should ensure the Notice Address is accurate and current. This section specifies how all official written communications related to the lease shall be delivered to either party. It also includes the parties' addresses and sometimes email addresses.

Notice – This section describes how any notice will be communicated to the lessor or the lessee, including certified mail, overnight delivery services, and electronic mail.

Destruction of Premises – Provides for termination of the lease by the lessee if destruction to the lessor's property prevents the lessee from using the property as outlined in the lease terms.

Condemnation – Provides the terms under which a lessee may terminate the lease should a condemning authority seize the lessor's property or a portion of the lessor's property, making the lessee's intended use no longer possible.

Abandonment – Provides the terms under which the site is defined as abandoned, either because of an abandoned tower or no site activity for a pre-defined period. This is typically three to five years.

Upon lapse of the pre-defined period, if a lessee abandons the site, the rights to the site may return to the lessor. In that case, if the tower and equipment have not yet been removed, it is possible that the lessee could be liable for unpaid rent and the total cost of site cleanup (often including a return to the previous condition except for normal wear and tear).

Insurance and Indemnification – This section outlines the required insurance and policy limits to be provided by the lessee and names the lessor as additional insured for liability coverage amounts ranging from as little as $500,000 to as much as $5,000,000 or more. Required policies often include commercial general liability, automobile liability, workers' compensation, and employer's liability.

Sometimes, the lessee may have the right to self-insure (typically subject to lessor approval). In most cases, the lessee will indemnify and hold harmless the lessor, its agents, officers, and employees from all claims, liabilities, obligations, or actions filed against the lessee arising from negligence or willful misconduct.

The lessee may also be obligated to defend the lessor against any action filed against the lessee for claims, liabilities, obligations, or actions and pay all reasonable costs and expenses. These may include any lessor fees incurred concerning the aforementioned items. This process is referred to as "indemnification."

Assignment – The lessee may assign a lease with the lessor's approval, which—in most instances—may not be unreasonably withheld. The act of assigning a lease usually involves the possibility of the lessee selling the lease rights to a third party at some point in the future.

Any transfer should be strict. I recommend that the lessor require the lessee to remain a party to the lease unless the party to whom the lease is assigned is a subsidiary (or closely connected) with similar financial capacity as the original lessee.

Such assignments also often involve review and negotiation by the lessor. That may include the cost of the lessor's attorney, the lessor's consultant, etc. I'd recommend seeking reasonable review fees payable to the lessor (typically up to $5,000 in 2023) before approving such a request. Such language should be included in the lease or a subsequent amendment or extension if possible.

Any assignment contemplated by the lessor will typically occur in conjunction with a lease and/or property sale, which will be discussed separately under the "Right of First Refusal" ("RoFR") section of this chapter and again in Chapter 7.

Sublease to Other Parties – This section can vary from lease to lease and may be absent altogether (especially on water towers, rooftops, or other utility structures). Effectively, this section aims to define a sublease by the lessee or the lessor to another lessee, as well as the rules, restrictions, and limitations for doing so. It may also cover the terms by which either the lessor and/or lessee will receive compensation because of such a sublease and the rights and privileges enjoyed by either or both for such a provision. Also, see "Revenue Sharing" and "Collocates."

Any proposed sublease application may include a nominal review fee, depending on the original lease. However, as I recommend in the case of an assignment by a lessee, it is often appropriate to charge a fee for the lessor's review of any lease amendment for a lessee or proposed sublessee. Even if a lease is already active, extension and amendment opportunities usually occur every few years. <u>Extensions and amendments are opportunities for the lessor.</u>

Title – The lessor is asked to represent (a claim to induce) and warranty (a promise) to the lessee that, as of the execution date of the lease, the title is sound with no defects, judgments, or liens. The lessor is also asked to further covenant (a solemn promise in writing that is signed, sealed, and delivered with a pledge of truth) that during the term of the lease, the lessor shall maintain good and valuable title and that the lessor has the full authority to execute the lease agreement. Further, the lessor covenants that no easements, restrictions, or prohibitions of use or occupancy exist that would prevent the lessee from using the premises as outlined in the lease.

Quiet Enjoyment – The Lessor agrees that the lessee shall have the right to the unimpaired use and enjoyment of the property according to the lease terms, subject to the lessee's payment of the agreed upon rent in a timely fashion. Quiet enjoyment may be implied in the lease even if an express clause is not included.

Repairs – This section allocates the responsibilities for any repairs required on the premises. Typically, the lessee is to keep all the lessee's equipment located on the premises in sound and structurally safe condition and in good repair and to be solely responsible for any expense associated with the repair and maintenance of said equipment. The lessor will often assume responsibility for maintaining the property as a whole—especially for anything that might interfere with or affect the lessee's access to any leased areas or easements.

Environmental – This section is used to verify the lessor's representations that the premises have not been, and are not currently used for, the generation, storage treatment, or disposal of hazardous materials, hazardous substances, hazardous wastes, pollutants, asbestos, polychlorinated biphenyls (PCBs), petroleum, or other fuels or underground storage tanks located on or near the premises.

The lessor can be held liable if any such representations are untrue. This clause also includes an indemnification provision that places liability for pre-existing conditions on the lessor and liability on the tenant for anything it or its agents or invitees bring to the site.

Default – Provides remedies if one of the parties does not fulfill one or more lease agreement details. Default on the lessor's part may include disruption of the tenant, not providing adequate access to the tenant, vandalism due to negligence, failure to pay property taxes, failure to pay the mortgage, and so on.

Default on the lessee's part includes failure to pay rent, disruption of other tenants, encroachment, failure to provide or pay for utilities, unauthorized use of equipment, and so on.

Mailing Address for Lease Payments – The address to which all lease payments are to be mailed. This may be different from the *Notice Address*.

Severability Clause – States that should any provision(s) of the lease be determined to be void, invalid, illegal, or unenforceable for any reason, such provision(s) shall be null and void. It also states that all other lease provisions shall be unaffected and remain valid and enforceable.

Governing Law – Identifies any local, state, or federal laws operative that govern the legal interpretation of the lease, and it identifies the court, legal jurisdiction, or authority for mediating or adjudicating a dispute between lessor and lessee, should one arise.

Terms or Conditions that Survive Lease Termination, Cancelation, or Expiration – Although it may appear odd at first glance, there may be lease elements that survive the life of the lease. These include representations, warranties, or other items that may affect future lessors. These are often defined for a specific period, although some are not subject to a specified time limit. You should consider applicable statutes of limitation.

SNDA (Subordination, Non-disturbance, and Attornment Agreement) – A subordination, non-disturbance, and attornment agreement (SNDA) addresses the priority of the rights of the tenant and any lenders. It deals with how and when the rights of the lessee will be subordinate to the rights of the lenders or, sometimes at the lender's option, senior to the lender's rights. The non-disturbance portion assures the lessee that its rights to the premises will be preserved ("non-disturbed") on specified conditions within the lessee's control, even if the lessor defaults on its loan and the lender forecloses.

The attornment component of the SNDA agreement states that the lessee will be permitted to continue its operations if a new lessor assumes the lease. It may also specify that the lender or lessor will have certain rights thereafter. It generally assures a lender that the lessee will attorn to (that is, confirm privity of contract by agreeing to continue as the lessee of the new lessor) the lender or a purchaser following a foreclosure. An SNDA agreement may also include other provisions for confirming or modifying further rights and obligations.

In the case of a cell tower lessee, an SNDA will preserve its right to remain on the property in the event of foreclosure. This right is usually a consideration when a lender has priority relative to the cell tower and the cell tower lease. It is used to prevent the cell tower lessee from being evicted from the property in the event a foreclosure of the property occurs.

Vandalism – Identifies which party is responsible for any vandalism and associated repairs and the terms, conditions, timeframes, and notice requirements.

Alarm System – Identifies the party responsible for providing an alarm system and monitoring. In some instances, I've observed requests by a lessee for the lessor to provide additional fencing or otherwise to secure the identified areas subject to the lease.

Fencing – Just as with the tower, equipment, antenna, etc., most lessees will secure their sites with fencing, for which the maintenance and security should be well spelled out in the lease or license. This can be important if the site is designated a "high crime" area (which is quite common). The property owner bears a responsibility to ensure that such fencing is maintained and not vandalized.

No Representation or Other Agreement Provision – States that the drafted and executed document supersedes and invalidates any other written or oral agreements and that all agreements must be in writing. Be certain **to get everything spelled out in writing before executing a new lease, an amendment, an extension, or any other lease-related document requiring a signature. Verbal agreements or "promises" are almost always worthless!**

Permits – Identifies the party responsible for obtaining necessary government permits for equipment construction, transmission, upgrades, etc. This can include local government permits, permits from the FCC and the FAA, coastal permits, or other environmental permits as required for a given location.

Lessor Inspection – Allows the lessor to inspect the premises, the compound, the tower, and so on to determine lease compliance. These rights ensure that equipment is confined to the premises defined in the lease and that any equipment not contemplated by the lease—or otherwise approved by the lessor—is not present. Such inspection rights can be especially important for "Collocations" and "Revenue Sharing."

Emergency Contact Information – Phone numbers and email addresses of the lessee and the lessor in emergencies. If possible, a few contacts should be provided for each party to the lease.

Lessee's Avoidance of Disturbing Other Tenants – Outlines the lessee's permitted activities and limitations of those activities such that they will not unreasonably impact other lessees, the lessor, or any neighboring properties.

Lessee agrees not to Create or Permit a Nuisance or Illegal Activity – Lessee must stipulate that it will operate legally and respect surrounding property owners' rights to quiet enjoyment of their properties. Sometimes, the lessor must also stipulate the same or similar terms.

Signature Page – Page or page section for execution by lessor and lessee and often notarization of signatures. It may also include an acknowledgment that any signatories are authorized to sign on behalf of the lessor and/or lessee. In some jurisdictions, witnesses may also be required (even if the document is required to be notarized).

Notary – A notary, or "notary public," is a state-licensed official witness to document signings who verifies the identities of document signers to help deter fraud and identity theft.

A notarized document will contain the stamp and signature of the notary who witnessed the signing, which provides more legal weight than a document that has not been notarized. Document signings that often require the services of a notary include real estate deeds, affidavits, wills, trusts, real estate loan documents, easements, cell tower leases, memoranda of leases, and authorized powers of the lessor or agents of the lessor.

Survey – Used to indicate the property's location, property boundaries, and restrictions & conditions that may apply to the legal description, measurement of land dimensions (in acreage or square feet), altitude, and the precise locations of any improvements on the property. In the case of a cell tower lease, the survey will include the tower and other infrastructure, equipment, and easements. Surveys will also help determine the presence of encroachments, inaccuracies, or possible title defects.

Legal Description – A written description that delineates a specific real property. It may be in the form of a metes and bounds description, a description by lot, block & section, and/or as a part of a platted subdivision or a subdivision map.

Description of Premises – The lessee's lease compound and equipment may include descriptions of any access and utility easements. This should not be confused with "Property."

Memorandum of Lease – A memorandum of lease or short-form lease ("MOL") is a very short document often recorded by the local county recorder/county clerk to notify others about the presence of—in this case—a cell tower lease affecting a property. MOLs are generally one to five pages long, depending on the lease's complexity and the jurisdiction in which the premises are located.

The MOL contains only the most critical, but not confidential, lease provisions. Usual inclusions are a description of the premises, the lease term, renewal rights, rights of first refusal, and exclusive use clauses. An MOL is recorded wherever deeds are recorded, and the recording fees are typically paid either by the party designated in the lease or, if not so designated, by the party requesting the recordation of the MOL.

The MOL's general purpose is to notify the world of the presence of the lease, which affects the property.

Monthly or Periodic Payments – Payments are often paid monthly to lessors during the lease term, although quarterly and annual payments are also common. Payments often range from a few hundred dollars to tens of thousands per month, depending on various factors. Multiples of a monthly payment will be paid if quarterly or annual payments are contractually agreed.

Annual or Periodic Escalators – Nearly every cell tower lease in the U.S. contains an escalator to mitigate the effects of inflation on lease payments. Although a few leases contain no escalators, the vast majority do. The escalators often range from 1 percent to 6 percent yearly or between 10 percent and 20 percent every five years.

While most escalators fall in the middle of the above ranges, leases containing escalators ranging from 10 percent to 15 percent per five years and 2 percent to 4 percent per year are the norm. Many leases provide an annual or periodic CPI ("Consumer Price Index") escalator, usually tied to one of the Bureau of Labor Statistics indices. A CPI escalator may be in conjunction with, or in place of, a fixed rate escalator.

CPI escalators are designed to adjust lease payments according to government-published inflation rates. This assures the lessor that income from the lease won't diminish (relative to published inflation) and that a lease won't become less valuable as the lease term continues.

Using the same logic, we can see that escalators that do not guarantee a minimum annual increase may cause a lease's equity value to diminish as the lease continues, especially when escalators are very low relative to CPI (as was the case for most cell tower leases during 2022).

By contrast, a large minority of leases contain annual escalators above 3 percent per year. This can create a scenario in which a lease payment will increase at a rate greater than historic CPI in the long term, thereby causing the lease to become more valuable to the lessor and more expensive to the lessee (often triggering a call by the lessee for optimization sooner rather than later). Before 2022, CPI was very low relative to most fixed lease escalators during most years, depending on the CPI used. Of course, there are several possible published indices from which to choose.

Right of First Refusal ("RoFR") – A Right of First Refusal states that if the lessor receives any offer to purchase the property or lease at any time after lease ratification, the lessee will have the right to match the price and terms of the offer accepted by the lessor within a given period (usually 30 days).

In all, there are a few types of RoFRs. Some are more restrictive than others, especially considering who the purchasing party is and whether the sale is for the lease, the land, or both.

The most restrictive RoFRs are known as "consent RoFRS" and generally provide the lessee with the right to refuse to permit the lease sale apart and separate from the underlying property or to a third-party aggregator.

RoFRs always require the lessor to provide legal notice to the lessee, which must be performed precisely. **<u>PLEASE BE CAREFUL WITH RoFRs.</u>**

Collocates – Collocates (or "Colocates") describe an instance where two or more lessees exist on the same cell tower, water tower, rooftop, or other wireless installation or compound.

In some instances, collocations may occur on the ground when a lessee has control of the tower but does not have enough ground space to meet the needs of additional ground tenants. This typically occurs when there are multiple tower tenants but a limited tower compound area.

Revenue Sharing – Otherwise known as "rev share" or "rev sharing," this section of a cell tower lease spells out the terms by which a lessor is to receive a portion of the rent paid by the lessee(s) and/or sub-lessee(s) for the tower, rooftop, and/or ground space. It almost always occurs only in an instance in which there are two or more lessees. While this is an important section, it must be well-understood and well-negotiated, as many opportunities exist for confusing language and misunderstandings. **Lessor audit rights are also very important here.**

Utility Reimbursement – Most U.S. cell tower leases have a provision for reimbursement or direct payment of utilities by the lessee. Lessees are typically required to provide their utilities, install a sub-meter, or reimburse the lessor for the utility costs.

If the lessee does not secure utilities, any utility billing reimbursement processes may need to be managed by the lessor monthly or quarterly to ensure that the lessee makes timely reimbursement payments. Reimbursement management costs should also be billed to the lessee.

Property Tax Reimbursement – Most U.S. cell tower leases have a provision for the lessor to be reimbursed for either: 1) a proportionate share of the property taxes based on the size of the leased area relative to the property size, or 2) a provable increase in property taxes due to the lessee's tower, equipment, or fixtures.

Lease Duration – Usually defined as the total of all lease terms, including the initial due diligence period, the first lease term, and subsequent option terms. The total lease duration typically exceeds twenty years and may often reach fifty years (though most are between twenty-five and thirty-five years from the lease effective or commencement date).

Perpetual Easement – This involves the perpetual right of use over, under, or through the property of another. This section outlines any approved equipment and restrictions of the easement's uses, hours, and expansions. Some agencies consider this a *de facto* subdivision, so a perpetual easement may not be permitted. Such easements are useful in the public right-of-way and for applications such as utilities, cell towers, or other uses where full-time habitation is not required.

Long-Term Lease – A lease longer than five or ten years, depending on the asset type. In the case of a cell tower lease, a long-term lease is usually the term applied for leases with a total duration between twenty years and fifty years (or more), including all option periods.

Equipment Removal – Upon termination of any cell tower lease, lessee equipment and improvements will require removal. I cannot emphasize enough the importance of including language to outline lessee responsibilities once a site is decommissioned. Such language should be inserted into the body of the lease when originally executed or when the carrier or tower company is seeking an amendment or extension that is not already incorporated into the lease. Here's an example of an Equipment Removal clause:

> *"The Premises shall be returned to its original condition, subject to normal wear and tear, within 30 days of lease termination, including the removal of all transmission equipment, towers, antenna, foundations, fencing, and any other remaining debris that was associated with the Lessee's use of the property."*

In addition to the above, please see the following section entitled "Holdover," which discusses rent continuation until the "Equipment Removal" terms have been satisfied by the lessee.

Holdover – The holdover clause defines the penalties the lessee will incur if the lessee occupies any leased area after lease expiration. The holdover clause will also outline the remedies for the lessor if the lessee stays in the property after lease expiration. Most holdover clauses define what a lessee must do to prevent triggering the holdover clause, such as the conditions outlined in the "Equipment Removal" clause above.

Holdover clauses will also include the rent cost during the holdover period, which can often be 100 percent, 150 percent, or even 200 percent of the rent paid in the month or term immediately preceding the expiration of the lease.

Holdover clauses will also reference sub-lessees, if any, or if sub-lessee presence was contemplated originally. Sub-lessees may not have the same rights or be subject to the same penalties as the lessee and may be subject to some form of damages.

Terms, Duration, and Modifications to a Lease Structure – After the original lease execution, from time to time, the lessee may request an amendment, an addendum, a modification, an upgrade, or an extension of the lease duration.

Such changes to the original lease may or may not trigger a rent increase or change(s) to the original lease terms.

Lease Amendments – Lease amendments are modifications to lease terms, often requested by the lessee, and may occur along with a lease extension. In cell tower leases, it is common for the lessee to begin to renegotiate lease terms many years before the expiration of the lease.

The items subject to negotiation are nearly endless but typically involve rent, escalator, number of lease terms, RoFR, property taxes, land area, collocation, revenue sharing, use, non-compete, and more.

A lessor unfamiliar with lease amendments will likely give away items of significant value and should always seek the advice of a qualified professional, just as when receiving a ground lease proposal or ground lease buyout proposal. **Lease amendments can significantly impact lease equity values (even if the payment and escalator terms remain the same or increase).**

Lease Extensions – As mentioned previously, most cell tower leases negotiated recently in the U.S. are structured with one or two 6-month to 12-month option periods, an initial 5-10-year lease period, and several 5-year options (often totaling thirty to fifty years or more). The lessee must exercise the lease extension before a given lease period ends to guarantee continued tenancy rights.

Unlike typical NNN commercial leases in which the value of the property is, relatively speaking, closely tied to the quality and total duration of lease tenants (longer is better), cell tower leases often work inversely. The less time remaining on a cell tower lease, the more valuable the lease may become to the lessor. This is largely due to the cost of taking down a tower, relocating any tower and ground lessees, then permitting and constructing a replacement tower (if no suitable alternatives exist).

Unlike option periods (typically included in the original lease terms), negotiating lease extensions is wide open. They give the lessor a negotiating advantage and the ability to seek (and obtain) a wide variety of concessions from the lessee. Like lease amendments, **lease extensions can significantly impact lease equity values (even in cases where the payment and escalator remain the status quo).**

Successor Leases (and Successor Lease Rights) – Successor Leases and Successor Lease Rights apply to the period beyond the end of the existing lease term (including the total of all remaining option terms), which may be exercised by the owner of a lease (or owner of the lease rights) to negotiate additional lease periods. An example is as follows:

Mr. Smith has a cell tower lease with a total remaining duration (including all option periods) of twenty-five years.

Mr. Smith sells his lease rights to a lease aggregator. The aggregator purchases Mr. Smith's lease rights for ninety-nine years, which means that the aggregator purchases the current lease and option terms and the rights to seventy-four years of successor lease terms. This period extends beyond the end of the current lease.

Author's Note: While it may appear easy to interpret and negotiate leases when the terms are spelled out clearly, most leases are proprietary. As such, they've been used thousands of times and are well-crafted to maintain lessee advantage from the start.

While one may assume that an experienced attorney will correctly anticipate and identify cell tower lease pitfalls, it is recommended that—in conjunction with an attorney—you hire a competent cell tower lease consultant to help identify "business strategic issues" within the lease and let the attorney focus on the "legalese" and any jurisdiction-specific legal considerations.

CHAPTER 6
CELL TOWER LEASE
VALUATION VARIABLES

This chapter includes a list of variables that should be considered when negotiating the sale of cell tower lease rights, a new cell tower lease, a cell tower lease extension, or an amendment to a cell tower lease.

While these points are valuable, I still recommend securing a qualified lease consultant to complete a negotiation on your behalf. This book will serve as a guide to familiarize you with the process, industry terms, and methods, but it is not designed to make you an expert on cell tower lease negotiations.

Just as the previous chapter discussed the illiteracy of real estate and legal experts concerning the methods used to calculate cell tower lease values, this chapter will expose the myriad of variables often overlooked by lessors, prospective buyers, property managers, and brokers.

CURRENT RENT

Current rent is the rent the lessee pays the lessor for the cell tower lease. It is often one of the primary factors used in determining lease value. Current rent is important when negotiating a lease extension or a lease buyout. After all, the difference between existing and appropriate site/market rent can greatly affect the amount received.

If the current lease rate is appropriate for the market (usually determined by a site and market analysis), then other variables should become the focus of the negotiation. In either case, a low lease rate does not *necessarily* indicate a low lease equity value (or sale price).

Telltale signs of significant upside rent potential include:

- An expanded compound area

- Any equipment additions or upgrades

- Additional tenants

- A poorly negotiated lease and/or lease amendments (which may be obvious because of rent, escalator, or lack of rev share/collocation rights)

Many overlook the upside and limitations imposed by a poorly negotiated lease at the outset. Such a factor, when properly understood, may become one of the best opportunities for the lessor when the time for a lease renewal, amendment, or extension approaches.

PERIODIC OR ANNUAL ESCALATORS

Periodic or annual escalators can be another one of the main lease value drivers, especially when the escalator is higher than the historic *CPI* rates.

For example, the difference between a lease with a 5 percent annual escalator and a 3 percent annual escalator can be tremendous over a long period. The 5 percent annual escalator increases the lease payment at about 1.67 times the rate of the 3 percent escalator annually. The following table illustrates this effect:

	5% Annual Escalator	3% Annual Escalator	Cumulative Difference
Rent (Year 1)	$24,000	$24,000	Zero
Rent (Year 6)	30,631	27,823	10.0%/$2,808
Rent (Year 11)	39,093	32,254	21.2%/$6,839

As time passes, you'll notice that the spread between annual rent values received for a lease with a 5 percent escalator versus the same lease with a 3 percent escalator increases. It is also important to realize that periodic escalators are not equivalent to annual escalators because the increase usually occurs every five years rather than yearly. As such, a 15 percent increase in rent rate every five years is not the same as a 3 percent increase yearly. The 3 percent increase yearly has compounded four times by the time year five comes along, resulting in a greater cumulative rent increase during the same 5-year period. This increase is also compounded as it carries forward.

The following table shows that the income created by the 15 percent escalator in the first 5-year term equals only 94 percent of the income created by the 3 percent annual escalator during the same period and just 92 percent over thirty years. The table outlines the above difference for a starting $10,000 annual payment **expressed at the end of each 5-year term:**

Term	Cumulative Rent	Escalator	Cumulative Rent	Escalator
5 Years	$53,091	3% annually	$50,000	15% per five years

Term	Cumulative Rent	Escalator	Cumulative Rent	Escalator
10 Years	114,639		107,500	
15 Years	185,989		173,625	
20 Years	268,704		249,669	
25 Years	364,593		337,119	
30-Year Total	**$475,754**		**$437,687**	

While the difference between a 3 percent annual escalator and a 15 percent 5-year escalator is somewhat nominal relative to the difference between a 5 percent annual escalator and a 3 percent annual escalator, it does add up over time.

When negotiating an annual escalator, I usually recommend that lessors seek a combination of CPI + 1 percent with a guaranteed minimum of 3 percent annually (or something with a reasonable rate floor). This way (in this example), one assures a minimum of 3 percent per year and will receive more if CPI exceeds the guaranteed 3 percent.

The same concept can be negotiated with a periodic escalator. Still, the recommended escalator will be the greater of 15 percent (as a rate floor), or the cumulative CPI for the immediately preceding 5-year period plus 1 percent.

Note: The market may not always support these examples. One must consider one's negotiating leverage for a new tower versus a lease extension or successor lease. Latter alternatives typically favor the lessor. One should expect a lessee to require a rate maximum ("cap") if a rate floor is negotiated.

REMAINING LEASE DURATION

In most areas of real estate, it is generally more desirable to have long-term leases. Regarding cell tower leases, it is often advantageous for lessors to renegotiate lease terms when less than five years remain in the final extension term. More favorable lease terms can be achieved, and such leases may command the greatest value from the lessee or, in the case of a lease sale, the market.

This single variable can be a primary indicator of value when renegotiating if there is a short time remaining and the lessee has no viable alternatives (especially with multiple tenants). Without a RoFR, the monthly lease rate and lease sale value may increase exponentially.

When the remaining lease duration is five years or less, lessees can get nervous, especially if the tower is in an area where relocating multiple lessee tenants poses a great risk. In that case, it can cost much more than just the new tower. In those situations, cell tower lessors have an opportunity to thrive.

It should be noted that if a single-tenant tower becomes short-dated (less than five years remaining in the final lease term), some of the leverage enjoyed by short-dated, multi-tenant brethren may not exist. Landlords may not enjoy the same negotiating leverage with single-tenant towers and should proceed cautiously.

TENANT QUALITY

There are different categories of cell tower and ground lessees, and the quality of each tenant to the lease market is based on its credit rating, market cap, and current, recent, or expected SEC filings, among other things.

Currently, most professionals in the wireless industry consider the top-tier lessees to be as follows:

- Verizon

- AT&T

- T-Mobile

- Dish*

- American Tower

- Crown Castle

- SBA Communications

- Vertical Bridge

Ground or tower leases with any of these companies, or a combination of these companies— all other things being equal—will be the most valuable to lease buyers. After all, these companies are publicly traded and are considered superior tenants relative to private companies, utilities, radio stations, or the local government.

* Dish lease sale values may not equal those of Verizon, T-Mobile, or AT&T. As Dish is new to the scene and has a relatively low market cap, lease buyers are not always as aggressive with Dish bids.

COLLOCATES

Collocates ("colos" or "collos") occur on a large percentage of cell towers and provide a great opportunity for the lessor—depending on the lease—to receive increased rents. They also allow the tower owner to achieve large profit margins and rents that may be greater than the base ground lease rent.

Consider this: I have personally negotiated a cell tower ground lease that previously paid the lessor less than $1,800/month and included a modest revenue-sharing provision. The lessee received about $18,000 monthly from the primary tenant and subtenants. We negotiated a new base rent of $3,500 monthly and 50 percent of everything over $8,000 monthly in current income. That resulted in $8,500 monthly rent to the lessor plus 3 percent annual escalators and guaranteed rent for ten years.

Many people in the industry consider collocates among the greatest potential sources of lessee profit, so I highly recommend that lessors pay close attention to this section of their lease. I also recommend paying close attention to the next topic—"Revenue Sharing."

REVENUE SHARING

Revenue sharing is the net benefit of collocates with a properly negotiated lease. It dictates the amount the lessor receives in a split with the lessee. I have observed splits that completely favored the lessee while others favored the lessor. There are several factors to consider when such negotiations are in play.

Seeking revenue share percentages above 50 percent is not recommended unless a thorough analysis of alternate and adjacent sites owned or operated by the same lessee has been conducted. If the revenue share is too high, the lessee may be disincentivized from aggressively marketing the site relative to alternative lessee sites, providing more favorable revenue opportunities. This may be true even when another tower requires upgrades to become a viable alternative for the lessee.

One other point that should be considered: The lessor should negotiate lease rate audit rights for any new terms or options, including rents currently being discussed (even if there is just one lessee). **This should always be negotiated with revenue sharing, expansion area, or collocation clauses.**

If the tower lease is in the final few years of the lease term, the likelihood of coming to terms on such a concession is very good. It can increase the current rent and lease equity value significantly.

EXPANSION AREA OPTION

It is common for a lessee to have an interest in acquiring additional land on an existing site such that they may be able to expand their offering and maximize their tower value. One should expect at least the same rent rate per square foot for an expansion area as for the initial area. That means (for example):

If a lessor receives $1,500 per month for a 1,000-square-foot ground lease area, and the lessee has the option to lease an additional 1,000 square feet of land, the land will be leased for the same $1,500 (plus cumulative escalator increases at the time the option is exercised). That means if the rent of the initial land area has increased over five years to $1,800 per month and the option is exercised at that time, the option areas will also be leased for $1,800 per month, bringing the total rent per month to $3,600.

While such an arrangement isn't necessarily bad, I recommend seeking to negotiate the lease of additional land at the time of a new lease, lease amendment, or revised lease extension. It's not just a future option for the tenant, which may never occur. The above example assumes that the existing lease rate has been analyzed and is at least consistent with recent market lease rates. It may occur depending on whether a lessee has a prospective tenant lined up.

In addition, one should be careful when defining "leased area" vs. "expansion area," vs. "property" vs. "option areas" vs. "other areas," and so on. Carriers, tower companies, and lease aggregators are masterful in using lease language and defined terms. Many lessors are not.

BUYER TYPE

Different buyer types (as previously discussed)—including tower companies, lease aggregators, private investors, and so on—have different criteria, standards, and motivations. For example, a private investor may prefer Verizon and AT&T leases and have little interest in Dish leases. In contrast, tower companies prefer to buy out their own leases, and lease aggregators will buy just about anything that makes sense.

LOCATION

"Location, location, location."

Just as in most areas of real estate, that saying may apply to cell towers and associated leases, but not necessarily for obvious reasons.

Limited existing and worthwhile tower and rooftop locations are available, especially in most high-density urban markets where space is at an ultra-premium and demand for signal, bandwidth, and users is ever-increasing. Remember that there is only so much room for antenna and towers—even with collos—while population and demand always increase. Currently constructed towers or antenna almost always have a significant advantage over the same or similar towers or antenna not yet constructed.

NON-COMPETE

A form of a restrictive covenant. Concerning cell tower leases, the right for an existing ground lease tenant to approve and/or control whether another tower is built on the property.

Be careful with non-compete clauses. To some lessors—someone with a cell tower consuming a small portion of their 10,000-square-foot lot, for instance—a non-compete clause will not likely create an issue. After all, there is little room to add another tower on the property.

However, if you own a multi-acre parcel and a carrier or tower company slips a non-compete clause into the lease, although they may only be leasing a 5,000-square-foot portion of your 50-acre parcel, the carrier or tower company may prevent you from leasing any land to a competing carrier or tower company.

These clauses should be eliminated, if possible.

ZONING

Zoning can determine almost everything about a property, including its value. In the case of cell towers, cities can use zoning ordinances to limit tower heights, restrict construction or use, implement safety precautions (such as fall zones), regulate aesthetics, and so on.

For tower companies, zoning restrictions can motivate them to work with other property owners in less restrictive environments with less "red tape" or cause them to modify an existing tower (if possible) instead of building a new one.

ADJACENT OR NEARBY TOWERS

The proximity of like-kind towers can harm the value of one, both, or several towers. After all, it creates redundancy. Carriers and tower companies dislike redundant towers unless growth in the covered area is projected to occur reasonably and at an acceptable rate.

One should make it a point to know the location and owners of nearby towers and their respective tenants. This information can improve one's understanding of tower company or carrier alternative sites and motivations. Refer to Appendix A for more information.

Remember, redundant towers can occur seemingly overnight (unless you maintain awareness of pending tower applications).

To illustrate, consider this potential scenario: One day, your neighbor Joe has a nice guyed tower on his ten acres with a few local tenants. The next day, a major public lessee buys the tower from Joe for a song so that a major lessee (or lessee from multiple other local/redundant towers) can move onto the tower—decommissioning two other nearby towers (including yours) in the process.

EXCESS CAPACITY

If a tower has the potential to add more tenants or equipment, that may provide additional value to a lessee. When speaking of excess capacity, I mean one or more of the following:

- **Structural Capacity:** Does a tower have excess capacity to support the weight of additional equipment?

- **Height:** Does a tower have excess height or space for additional lessees and/or equipment?

- **Ground Space:** Is there excess ground area adjacent to or surrounding a tower where additional equipment can be placed?

MERGERS AND ACQUISITIONS

An additional threat to site stability may come in the form of corporate consolidations, mergers, or acquisitions; these are almost always in the works on some level between carriers and tower companies to maximize efficiency, reduce OpEx and/or CapEx, and eliminate or reduce competition.

Such a scenario may result in the merger of two lessees, thereby eliminating redundant or otherwise unnecessary towers (unless such a merger occurs on the lessor's tower instead of away from it). Unlike single-site decommissioning due to financial considerations, depending on how the site fits into the proposed network, site-specific costs may be trumped by network deployment needs for which there may be little need to negotiate with the lessor.

When AT&T attempted to acquire T-Mobile several years ago, the lease purchase market reacted strongly based on the rumors alone. Suddenly, lease buyers speculated on the value of T-Mobile and AT&T leases near one another. Many buyers became much more selective in the buyout of leases for either carrier until the merger was finalized or canceled.

As it happened, the deal was never concluded, so things quickly returned to normal. However, the scenario showed how quickly the market can respond to uncertainty in this area.

More recently, as most people realize, Sprint was acquired by T-Mobile in one of the largest mergers in the history of U.S. wireless and created the largest wireless carrier in terms of market cap in the United States (leapfrogging both AT&T and Verizon in the process).

Although it is difficult to predict who will merge with whom (or if the Department of Justice will permit any more), who will acquire the towers of whom, and how the market will respond, it is safe to say that as technology changes and the industry evolves, cell tower decommissioning will remain a fact of life.

TERM TO BE SOLD

The value of any cell tower lease sale is largely determined according to the length of the time being sold. It may be the only variable that is linear in nature.

For example, if a lessor were to sell ten years of future cash flows, the amount received would be nowhere near the amount the same lessor could receive for the same lease, with the same terms and carrier mix, if the lease cash flows were sold for ninety-nine years or as a perpetual easement.

Unlike other variables of a lessor's cell tower lease sale (such as rent, escalator, etc.), the term to be sold may be one of the few variables the lessor has nearly absolute discretion and control over at the time of the lease sale.

This variable should not be confused with the remaining lease duration.

PREPAID LEASE

Relative to a long-term lease or perpetual easement, prepaid leases are often limited to the current and existing lease extension terms. These amount to something between ten and fifty years (although other options are known to exist), depending on the remaining lease duration and including all options. The lessor is simply selling lease cash flows in advance at a discount rate offered by the lessee, the ground tenant, and the tower owner.

While the upside is additional financial security for the lessor, it is not without its downsides. First, income taxes from the sale may be based on the amount received, and an acceleration of the lease payments may be subject to taxation at ordinary income rates (depending on various factors).

Second, most often, such a sale will be limited to the lessee who owns the tower (although not all tower owners are interested in prepaying leases in place of an easement). Most third parties will not be interested in making an offer without an easement. Such a scenario largely eliminates any future upside to third-party buyers by limiting the terms sold to the cashflows only, as opposed to rights to the existing and expansion areas (which can be leased to new tenants or the ground lease tenant if such an opportunity were to present itself).

Finally, unlike an easement, prepaid leases will not likely qualify for a 1031 exchange. I'll discuss the above-referenced topics in Chapter 10.

LONG-TERM LEASE

A long-term lease is like a standard ground lease, except that the lessor may enter into a lease with options totaling fifty years or more, as opposed to the typical twenty-five to thirty-five years.

However, unlike a prepaid lease, the lessor will retain the risk of lease termination, as with the standard cell tower lease.

Long-term leases may be prepaid or the rights sold to a lease aggregator (or other investors). Usually, they comprise an additional series of lease term extensions requested by the lessee to provide them with the greatest potential benefit while retaining the flexibility to cancel the lease with little notice and any or no reason.

Often, these additional option periods are "offered" in conjunction with the tenant exercising a lease extension. The lessee may even offer a nominal fee to the lessor for agreeing to such an extension.

I always recommend against a lessor agreeing to any form of a long-term lease or extension of lease periods. The reason is that it creates several unintended consequences:

- It reduces the incentive for the lessee to negotiate on any lease points for years to come;

- It decreases the lease sale value to the lessor;

- It reduces the value to lease aggregators and the lease buyout market, as one of their primary sources of income is based on a buyer's ability to renegotiate lease rates and terms;

- It provides little, if any, additional benefit to the lessor (additional option periods are just that—options to be exercised by the lessee while providing the lessor nothing in return until, and only if, an option is exercised),

- And it does nothing, by itself, to eliminate a lessee's right to early termination.

90

Generally, considering the above, I recommend that lease extensions are for no longer than twenty years (four 5-year options), with at least half of the extension term payments guaranteed. This type of negotiation can become quite complex and requires significant analysis of "lease versus sale."

PERPETUAL VERSUS TERM EASEMENTS

Forever.

That is what is being sold when a lessor sells a cell tower lease in exchange for a perpetual easement—much like subdividing and selling the leased area and with the same consequence as selling the leased area as fee-simple real estate.

Perpetual easements can be risky to the lessor and should be understood before entering such an agreement. A perpetual easement can burden a property in ways that can make a subdivision and sale or future development problematic.

On the other hand, term easements are structured with a limit to the amount of time being sold, typically from as few as ten years to as many as ninety-nine years. SteepSteel often advises government, utility, church, or non-profit clients interested in selling a lease to sell in the form of a term easement—usually between thirty and sixty years—as tax-exempt sellers are not typically subject to any income tax on the sale.

Another obvious advantage to selling leases in exchange for a term easement is that the easement will terminate at some future date, and the property will revert to the seller (assuming the site is still active). This may allow for a repeat of the process (which will rarely happen if the lease is sold in perpetuity unless the site is abandoned or decommissioned).

I also point out to my clients that the sale of a lease on a fifty-year term basis, or more—when income tax consequences are not a consideration—usually provides the seller nearly the same sale value as a perpetual easement in terms of revenue at closing.

LUMP SUM VERSUS INSTALLMENTS

A lump sum means payment in full today. Therefore, it poses no risk to the lessor.

Installments, on the other hand, mean ongoing payments. Payments for a term easement or perpetual easement still contain the risk inherent in any associated installment agreements, as carriers, tower companies, and aggregators do go out of business, file bankruptcy, consolidate, merge, and so on.

While an early cancelation provision may no longer be an issue —depending on who your agreement is with—until the check clears the bank, there is the possibility that future payments will not be paid to the seller once an installment agreement is made. That's regardless of any "guarantees" to the contrary.

If, for example, a publicly traded lessee offers a seller between five and fifteen years of installment payments, given the history of the wireless telecommunications industry, the risk of loss is far less than the industry average decommission risk (especially in the case of a single-tenant tower). When one combines that with the potential income tax savings of spreading the payments over several years as opposed to one lump sum, it might make financial sense.

I do not recommend clients consider an installment sale with any buyer other than a publicly traded tower company.

RIGHT OF FIRST REFUSAL

Some prospective commercial property buyers will not go through the exercise to prepare an offer on a property if the property is subject to a Right of First Refusal ("RoFR"). That's because drafting offers on commercial real estate can become expensive and time-consuming and may involve the use of an attorney.

Since most residential transactions are not as complicated as their commercial counterparts, offers and negotiations can often be handled exclusively by agents or brokers without attorneys. Despite this fact, as most buyers are unfamiliar with cell towers and cell tower leases, buyers often get confused by the tower (first) and discouraged by the RoFR (second). Therefore, buyers may not be as likely to write an offer. Even those who understand cell towers and cell tower leases will often avoid making offers on properties subject to RoFRs as the effort may prove fruitless.

In effect, RoFRs can reduce buyer interest in cell tower-related properties. At a minimum, this can reduce a given property's sale value or increase the time required to sell in an otherwise competitive market.

It is also worth noting that there are different types of RoFRs, such as those which apply to:

- Offers for the entire property (with or without the lease);

- Offers for the lease, or leases, only;

- Offers from different buyer types (such as aggregators);

- and more.

Finally, there are RoFRs that require the approval of the lessee. This is not the same as matching the offer and can be the most problematic, as a denial by the lessee may stop the sale of a lease entirely or require that the underlying property be sold in conjunction with the lease.

Not all RoFRs are created equal. Some have more teeth than others. As such, be careful when permitting a RoFR in a new lease. If a lessee will not execute a lease without a RoFR, the language in the RoFR should be narrow in scope. It should also include a short response duration in the event of an offer and be specific to the sale type (property, lease, both, etc.) within the scope of the RoFR. Finally, I recommend that RoFRs have sunset clauses, if possible.

COSTS FOR A TOWER COMPANY TO RELOCATE A TOWER

Lessors should try to educate themselves about rents paid to the tower company by any sub-lessees that may be on the tower. While obtaining this information may be difficult, lease consultants and data managers can assist.

It is often the case that towers with multiple tenants must provide the lessor with tower rent information as a condition of revenue sharing or collocation clauses contained in the ground lease. This may only happen if you ask, however.

When dealing with any tower owner during a lease renegotiation, extension, or amendment—especially tower company lessees whose tower contains one or more collocates—the true potential value of the lease can be significantly more than just paying the cost of a new tower.

In addition to the cost of a new tower, there will be a cost for taking the old tower down (perhaps even including foundation removal), a cost for relocating the lessees (which may not happen immediately, potentially requiring temporary solutions like

C.O.W.s or C.O.L.T.S.), and the potential for temporary or permanent revenue or tenant loss during the relocation if one or more lessees makes other arrangements.

Although lease buyers may try to sell you on the fact that the perpetual lump-sum payment is "only" worth $300,000 to them, based on 200+ times $1,500 per month (for example), if there are multiple tenants, you can bet a decommission has the potential to cost the lessee hundreds of thousands more than the $300,000 offered if no deal is made well in advance of lease expiration.

AGE OF LEASE

The current lease rate is not necessarily the defining factor regarding lease value. Most leases in their final term reach the pinnacle of their value relative to any other time in the lease life cycle (all other things being equal). This single variable can be the greatest indicator of value when renegotiating. If a short time remains and a lessee has no viable alternatives, the lease rental rate and sale value can increase exponentially.

With that in mind, one should realize that carriers and tower companies may have a Plan "B" if Plan "A" doesn't work, and their plans are often—but not always—a few years in the making. So, before you start telling the tower company "how it's gonna be" and "what it's going to cost them" (as I've heard people utter), please take a step back and think. Then, contact someone qualified to walk you through the process without losing your lease.

In addition to the above, there is something else you should know about:

REIMBURSABLES

These are the items most often overlooked by landlords and can include maintenance, property taxes, and utilities.

These items may not sound like much, but a cell single-tenant tower can run up a $1,000+ monthly electric bill. If a lessor has a carrier piggybacking without the lessor's knowledge on a large commercial multi-family property without separate meters, it can happen without the lessor realizing it.

Property tax reimbursements are often overlooked because lessors do not examine their property tax bill closely enough to understand what to look for, how to collect it, or what the lease says about such reimbursements.

When past due utilities or taxes are discovered, the damage could amount to tens of thousands of dollars or more after just a few years. As you can imagine, carriers balk—even if they are in the wrong—and when they do, it requires creative solutions to avoid going to court.

Instead of a lump-sum reimbursement, I typically recommend rewriting or amending the lease to increase rent along with a rent guarantee, then monetizing the amended lease based on the increased rental value.

CHAPTER 7
CELL TOWER LEASE
VALUATION METHODS

H aving reviewed thousands of cell tower leases, I can say that cell tower lease values may be the most misunderstood area of cell tower leases to those *outside* the industry. There are several reasons for this, not the least of which is the counterintuitive nature of leases. That said, the valuation *methods* are very straightforward.

The following methods for determining cell tower lease values are different ways of arriving at the same result. Some formulas and calculations are effectively identical to the methods used to analyze commercial or residential property values and similar cashflow-dependent investments. Regardless of the method chosen, professionals work with Microsoft Excel, industry finance software, or proprietary software and generally do not perform calculations on paper or in their heads.

In this chapter, I'll cover carrier, tower company, lease aggregator, and private individual lease valuation methods in a way that provides a basic understanding of the terms, how cell tower leases are analyzed, and how market lease values are established. I will not attempt to explain the subjective finance variables that vary from organization to organization, individual to individual, and market to market. My goal is to take the mystery out of the wireless telecom industry by explaining, in the simplest possible terms, how lease buyers establish values and what lessors should expect if cell tower lease valuations or monetizations become a part of their future.

As mentioned, cell tower leases are exceptional among real estate leases in that they can be appraised and sold independently of the underlying fee-simple real estate. That element will differentiate the accepted valuation methods for a property with an active, non-monetized cell tower lease from the accepted valuation methods of commercial or residential income properties without an active, non-monetized cell tower lease.

In most instances, residential and commercial income property leases dictate a given property's value based largely on the property's net operating income ("NOI") and the quality of the tenants. By contrast, the valuation of cell tower leases is strongly influenced by additional market and site-specific variables, so much so that the rent can be much less relevant to a lease's appraised value. That said, one should not rely exclusively on the value metrics considered for the underlying property when establishing the lease value and vice-versa.

That is not to say that cell tower lease values cannot be or never are used to determine a property's overall value. In fact, they are often included in calculating the property's value (especially when a lender will allow the lease to be considered part of a given property's collateral). Just because an appraiser decides that a cell tower lease should be included in an appraisal using the same valuation method or formula for the lease as for the remainder of the property or structures on the property does not make it correct.

Unfortunately, arbitrary cell tower lease values based on an estimated cap rate—or a cap rate assumed to be the same as the rest of the underlying property—often result in a great disservice to the property owner (and the buyer). For these reasons, a qualified individual or firm should appraise cell tower leases *separately* from the underlying real estate based also on industry, lease, and site-specific factors—not just real estate factors.

REAL ESTATE APPRAISALS VERSUS CELL TOWER LEASE APPRAISALS

It's worth noting that the income approach appraisal method, the cost approach appraisal method, and the comparison approach appraisal method (as historically conducted) are typically insufficient to determine a cell tower lease value.

Let's consider the reasons:

- There are too many non-real estate variables that must be considered when determining the present value of a cell tower lease;

- There are not adequate comps from which to draw (relative to fee-simple properties), and those that exist are not necessarily conclusive as to accurate "market" rent value;

- Lessee equipment/tower condition is not a factor, and

- The capitalization rate of the lease is likely different—perhaps very different—from that of the underlying real estate (especially when considering short-dated, multi-tenant leases).

- The cost of the tower and equipment are largely irrelevant to the lease value unless the lessor also owns the tower, in which case the tower value should be calculated as well. The ground and tower equipment are almost always the property of the lessee(s).

For example, a large public agency inquired about a cell tower lease valuation. One of their leases was with a major public tower company, and it happened to be on holdover with six tenants (including all the major carriers). The agency received approximately $5,500 per month for the tower and all the tenants, which would have equaled, in the case of an average market lease sale, perhaps $1.2 million to $1.4 million had the agency inadvertently extended the lease or asked a real estate appraiser to value the lease.

In this case, however, the *tower* ownership was supposed to revert to the agency upon the expiration of the ground lease. As it happened, the lease contained a reversion clause. Unbeknownst to the agency, that meant the agency effectively became the owner of a six-tenant, 280-foot cell tower (along with all lease rights) overnight. Such clauses are often not picked up by lessors or their agents.

A few months later, on behalf of the agency, we successfully auctioned the tower and the leases for $4.1 million. As mentioned previously, had the tower and leases been appraised using most standard formulas upon which appraisers rely, or had the agency inadvertently extended the ground lease, the agency would have left nearly $3 million.

As one can now see, the rent a cell tower generates is but one consideration in its ultimate sale value, and that's why, when people ask what their cell tower lease is worth, my standard response is, "That depends…"

LENDERS

Purchasers, sellers, or parties refinancing a property, including a cell tower, should understand that many lenders will not accept a cell tower lease as a portion of collateral for a loan. Many lenders have misconceptions about the risks associated with leases and towers. These problems can be overcome (often to the borrower's advantage). If you run into a situation where a cell tower lease will be used as collateral for a loan, please stop and seek qualified cell tower lease and real estate counsel.

If you require assistance with capitalization, monetization, management, consulting, or any other cell tower lease-related issues, visit **SteepSteel.com** and submit a request to contact you for a prompt reply.

Policies can vary greatly when purchasing a property, refinancing, or selling a cell tower lease absent the property ("Lease Stripping"). That's why an SNDA is an essential consideration. In any case, some solutions can involve moving to a different lender, financing, or refinancing a property without including the lease(s) as collateral, or—depending on your needs or the needs of the deal—selling the lease in conjunction with the property purchase.

LIVING DOCUMENTS

Cell tower leases are "living documents." The value of the lease can change dramatically based exclusively on the remaining duration of the lease. In most cell tower leases, the lease value increases—in addition to that which typically occurs because of the lease escalator or other organic factors—based on variables that *may not* otherwise be considered relevant.

The following should provide a basic understanding of how cell tower lease values are calculated but should not be considered exhaustive.

FINANCIAL CONCEPTS

The most basic concept associated with finance and investment is the Time Value of Money. It's a concept that states that any amount of money today is worth more than it will be tomorrow due to its interest-earning or compounding potential, risk, and inflation.

Time Value Money (TVM)

The following formula is the basis for calculating the future value of money to compare it to the present value:

$$FV = PV \times \backslash[1 + (i / n)\backslash] \wedge (n \times t)$$

$$PV = FV / \backslash[1 + (i / n)\backslash] \wedge (n \times t)$$

Where:

FV = the future value of money
PV = the present value
i = the interest rate or other return that can be earned on the money
t = the number of years to take into consideration
n = the number of compounding periods of interest per year

DCF (Discounted Cash Flow)

Discounted cash flow (DCF) is an analysis method used to value investment by discounting the estimated future cash flows.

Sample valuation formulas and methods are explained below:

An explanation of DCF analysis uses future free cash flow projections. DCF discounts the future cash flow projections to arrive at a present value used to evaluate the investment potential. If a project is financed using debt and equity, the weighted average cost of capital will often apply. The opportunity may be good if the value arrived at through DCF analysis is higher than the current investment cost.

The discounted cash flow formula is:

$$DCF = CF_1 / (1 + r)^1 + CF_2 / (1 + r)^2 + ... + CF_n / (1 + r)^n$$

Where:

CF = Cash Flow
r = discount rate
n = number of periods

The DCF formula can value any returns expected from an investment. The formula discounts each future cash flow at a rate that reflects the riskiness of the cash flow for the period in question.

DCF is calculated in the following example:

				start	start esc	4.0%	
			esc chg year:	10	new esc	4.0%	
Discount Rate	7.00%						

Year	Escalator	Revenues	Expenses	Net Revenue	Discount Factor	Annual	Cumulative
1	4.00%	$46,200	-	$46,200	0.9667	$44,663	$44,663
2	4.00%	$48,048	-	$48,048	0.9035	$43,411	$88,074
3	4.00%	$49,970	-	$49,970	0.8444	$42,194	$130,268
4	4.00%	$51,969	-	$51,969	0.7891	$41,011	$171,279
5	4.00%	$54,047	-	$54,047	0.7375	$39,861	$211,140
6	4.00%	$56,209	-	$56,209	0.6893	$38,743	$249,883
7	4.00%	$58,458	-	$58,458	0.6442	$37,657	$287,540
8	4.00%	$60,796	-	$60,796	0.6020	$36,601	$324,142
9	4.00%	$63,228	-	$63,228	0.5626	$35,575	$359,717
10	4.00%	$65,757	-	$65,757	0.5258	$34,578	$394,295

This DCF analysis is the basis for calculating the present value of the potential future value of the cash flows generated by a cell tower lease. Programs such as Excel can provide a simple method for making such calculations. They will quickly make sense of what might otherwise appear to be almost arbitrary cell tower lease valuations offered by lease buyers.

Below is a simple example of a DCF:

Current annual payment: $18,000
Escalators: 3% annually
Discount rate: 12%
Term: 30 years

The current value of all future cash flows for 30 years: $194,512

To put it another way:

- If a lessor was scheduled to receive $18,000 this year, *and*

- That amount was scheduled to increase at a rate of 3 percent annually for the next 30 years, *and*

- The cumulative amount to be received during the next 30 years was discounted back at 12 percent such that all future cash flows were received by the lessor today, *then...*

...the amount paid to the lessor would be equal to $194,512 now.

To illustrate the difference between a 12 percent discount rate and a 10 percent discount rate, we will apply the above formula to the following example:

- If a lessor was scheduled to receive $18,000 this year, *and*

- That amount was scheduled to escalate at a rate of 3 percent annually for the next 30 years, *and*

- The cumulative amount to be received during the next 30 years was discounted back at 10 percent such that all future cash flows were received by the lessor today, *then...*

...the amount paid to the lessor would be equal to $232,179.

As you can see, a change in the discount rate from 12 percent to 10 percent over the same period, with the same escalator and the same starting lease payment, causes the current value of the future cash flows to increase from the original $194,512 to $232,179. That's an increase of $37,667 (or nearly 20 percent) over the lease term.

This discount rate—and associated price—being offered in a lease sale is largely predicated on six variables:

1. The total cost of capital to the investor;

2. The remaining duration of the lease being purchased;

3. The potential lease upside in the near term and the long term;

4. The yield the investor requires;

5. The investment risk, and

6. The duration being sold.

If one wants to know the cumulative value of all cash flows over 30 years, one can simply eliminate the discount rate and see that the total revenue generated in thirty years equals $856,357. But that represents an amount that might not ever be received and would only occur if the lease remained active under the current terms for thirty years *and* the entirety of the payments due were paid as scheduled over the next thirty years.

Multiples
Multiples represent a quick and easy way to evaluate lease cash flow values and are sometimes expressed in ranges of value until specific lease factors, such as remaining lease duration, alternate sites, escalator, tenants, collocates, revenue share, reversion

clause, RoFR, length of time being offered for sale (for example thirty years, fifty years, ninety-nine years, perpetual), and option areas can be determined.

The formula for multiples is simple and is expressed as follows:

Monthly Lease Payment = MLP
Monthly Multiple = MM
Current Value = CV
MLP*MM = CV

So, if MLP = $1,500 and the MM = 180, the CV is expressed as $1,500 * 180 = $270,000

Depending on the above variables, the value of cell tower lease buyouts often ranges from as little as 30x to as much as 400x or more than the current monthly payments for a defined period. Multiples may also be expressed relative to annual income instead of monthly income, but the result will be the same.

Capitalization Rate

Capitalization rate ("Cap Rate") is a real estate valuation method used to compare investments. The cap rate is generally calculated as the annual net operating income ("NOI") generated by a real estate asset divided by its current market value (or the asking price before the sale).

In the case of cell tower leases, as they are triple net leases ("NNN"), no expenses get passed onto the lessor (unless otherwise specified), so the rent received by the lessor is usually equal to the NOI.

For example, if Steve buys a property that generates an NOI of $120,000 per year and pays $900,000, the cap rate is expressed as 120,000/900,000 or 13.33 percent.

To explain the cap rate further, let's consider the following comparison to better illustrate the point:

Property "A" has a $100,000 NOI with multiple investment-grade tenants. The investor's risk is low, so a 5 percent rate of return is deemed appropriate. If we divide the $100,000 by .05, the asset's value to the investor is $2,000,000.

Property "B" also has a $100,000 NOI with a single non-investment-grade tenant. The investor's risk is much higher, so the investor requires a 10 percent rate of return. If we divide $100,000 by .10, we find the asset's value to the investor is $1,000,000.

Cell tower lease values may also be expressed in cap rates by sellers or their brokers, indicating an incorrect lease sale value is also being applied to the lease and/or the total property value.

Remember, the cap rate is simply the NOI (or proforma NOI) divided by the advertised property's market value (or asking price). Here's an example:

NOI = $50,000
Property List Price (PLP) = $500,000
$50,000/$500,000 = .10, or 10%, or a "10 cap"

The inverse is also true as if a property is valued at $500,000 with a
$50,000 NOI, it is also a "10 cap"

Each lease valuation method discussed thus far will ultimately reach the same financial conclusion.

PROPRIETARY LEASE VALUE CONSIDERATIONS

While most lease buyers will speak to lessors regarding multiples or discount rates, the lease buyers' calculations are often based on a proprietary IRR or yield model that determines the range of lease purchase prices based on various known and unknown factors to the market.

It is critical to shop for cell tower lease offers among multiple qualified buyers. Many people in the industry will try to convince you that a lease is only worth "X" because that is what they are willing to pay. Still, it's important to remember that all investors have different motives, objectives, thresholds, costs of capital, debt and equity stacks, and circumstances driving their prices. This is why "market" lease values can vary dramatically.

CHAPTER 8
REAL ESTATE TRANSACTIONS
INVOLVING CELL TOWERS

I n this chapter, I will discuss what I believe to be the core interest of most *Cell Tower Secrets* readers. At the end of the day, most cell tower lease landlords will sell a cell tower lease-related property (or the lease itself) at some point.

This is where the real magic happens in this business. The carriers and tower companies don't realize it. Otherwise, they might have structured these leases differently from the beginning.... But, to the landlords' collective benefit, they didn't.

If landlords realize the mistakes to avoid, they can capitalize on real estate transactions involving cell tower leases.

THE REAL DEAL ON THE BENEFITS OF
CELL TOWER TRANSACTIONS

As one can imagine, when a property transaction includes a cell tower, it adds another layer of complexity. That's true whether it includes a property purchase or sale, a refinance, or a lease sale.

In addition to the financial benefits a cell tower lease provides, one must also consider the responsibilities associated with a property with a cell tower lease. That's because any management responsibilities will remain with the property whether the owner of the record is the same person who receives the cell tower lease payments.

As previously noted, cell tower lease rights can be sold in conjunction with or without the underlying property. The lessor may sell the lease rights and retain the property or sell the property and retain the lease rights. A lessor may also keep or sell both simultaneously.

For many lessors, the sale of cell tower lease rights alone can be an excellent source of capital. It can be a relatively simple process that provides an alternative to a loan against, or a sale of, the underlying property.

Another potential benefit of selling a cell tower lease while retaining the underlying property is receiving significant cash without creating a taxable event. If curious, consult your tax professional to see if this applies to your situation. On the other hand, selling a cell tower lease may create undesirable consequences when a property is sold separately. Read the Lease Stripping section later in this chapter for more information. Additionally, those consequences may be highlighted regarding a reduction in property value. For more information, read the Value Penalty section later in this chapter.

Regarding alternatives, when a property with a cell tower lease is sold, including just the property, the cell tower lease, or both, the lessor should seek a qualified lease consultant to determine the lease value. One should also secure the services of a competent real estate broker. These actions will help to determine the consequences and/or benefits of selling the lease or property separately or together.

The following sections, while a guide to the most likely transaction considerations, are not exhaustive.

EXTRA DUE DILIGENCE

The purchase or sale of a property, including or subject to a cell tower lease, creates extra due diligence for the buyer and extra disclosure for the seller. In either scenario, the cell tower lease can be a critical element, and both the seller and the buyer should make it a point to become familiar with the meaning of the lease terms. Likewise, they should be familiar with how those terms can affect, restrict, or impose additional responsibilities relative to the property on each party, especially in cases where there is a RoFR, an Option, a Revenue Sharing, or a Non-Compete clause in place.

PURCHASING A PROPERTY, INCLUDING A CELL TOWER LEASE

Purchasing a property with a cell tower lease is perhaps the most common way to become a cell tower lessor. If one understands the property value and the lease value, is comfortable with being a cell tower lessor, and can accept the potential risks associated with owning a property with a cell tower (especially if part of the property purchase was based on the cell tower lease value). One will likely enjoy the learning experience of this part of the transaction and the cell tower lessor experience overall.

As explained earlier, purchasing a property with an active cell tower lease is much the same as any real estate purchase, except that it involves extra due diligence. If one is comfortable evaluating an active cell tower lease without a cell tower lease consultant, the following is a minimum part of the due diligence. One should determine:

- Whether the cell tower lease payments are accurate and current, according to the lease and lease amendments.

- Whether a rent guarantee is in place, and understand the terms and potential consequences.

- What lease escalators exist, and are existing escalators reasonable relative to historical, current, and projected inflation? Otherwise, a lease value correction may be required.

- Whether—upon lease termination or expiration—the lessee is responsible for removing all equipment promptly, including the tower foundation.

- That any lessor responsibilities under the lease are reasonable and appropriate.

- That one fully understands the benefits and potential consequences of the lease.

- That no notices have been sent by the carrier, tower company, or an agent indicating an intent to decommission the tower, terminate the lease, or reduce the current or future rents or escalators.

- The tower and equipment have been surveyed, and there are no illegal encroachments to or from neighboring properties.

- That title insurance will include the fee property and any potential leasehold rights.

- The tower's presence does not preclude the property owner (or future property owners) from using and developing the remainder of the property according to its highest and best use.

- Ensure that the cell tower lease rights and future payments are transferred to the new property owner as of the closing date. Since the transfer of payments will likely require 60-90 days post-closing, the buyer should collect a seller credit equal to two cell tower lease payments at closing. If a tower is also included, seek the services of a competent lease consultant.

- That—especially in the case of a rooftop installation—the roof is well-maintained, has been engineered for the equipment already installed, and has no damage. I also recommend having the roof installation reviewed by a competent roofing contractor and the roof framing inspected by a licensed structural engineer. If a carrier or tower company provides a report from an engineer, have the report reviewed by another engineer tasked with ensuring that your best interests are protected.

If everything else checks out, the value of the cell tower lease should be at least equivalent to any premium included as part of the total purchase price. If financing, make certain the addition of the lease does not create a problem with the lender. Some lenders do not like to include cell tower leases as collateral for loans.

The due diligence period is also an opportune time to determine whether the sale of the lease cash flows can benefit the acquisition more than retaining the lease and lease cash flows. A discussion of lease cash flow sales at closing is beyond the scope of this book, but it can be managed by contacting a competent lease consultant and a qualified broker.

I have encountered hundreds of transactions in which the value of the cell tower lease (at property purchase) was equal to or greater than the property's asking price. While this scenario isn't typical—property sellers have recently become increasingly savvy about cell tower lease values—such scenarios were quite common only a few years ago. This is related to many brokers and property owners' lack of understanding about cell tower leases and their associated lease values. Due to this lack of understanding, it is common to find properties listed with over or under-market values when considering the lease value in the pricing equation.

PURCHASING A PROPERTY SUBJECT TO
A CELL TOWER LEASE OR EASEMENT

The purchase of a property on which a cell tower is constructed but provides no cash flows to the new lessor is commonly referred to as "subject to the lease" or "subject to an easement." It **does not** relieve the new property owner from the lessor responsibilities outlined in the lease.

Many people have the false impression that they will have no responsibility to the cell tower lease tenant when they purchase a property subject to a cell tower lease if such a purchase does not include lease payments. However, that is not the case.

When purchasing a property subject to a cell tower lease or easement, the prospective buyer should be certain that the lessor's responsibilities do not impose a cost on the lessor. They should also ensure that any such cost has been contemplated in the property purchase price unless reimbursable to the lessor under the lease.

Also, verify that the property appraiser understands and considers any value penalty of the tower on the property (considering the absence of lease payments). The value of a property with a cell tower and no payments can be lower than that of a comparable property without a cell tower (because of the tower's presence and associated opportunity costs). After all, the cell tower will occupy a portion of the property and could make the occupied portion of the property unusable for other purposes for many years.

While this may seem counterintuitive when purchasing a property, it is better to address this issue before purchase than to realize after closing that the purchase price was too much.

I refer to the above as a potential form of Value Penalty (which I've discussed throughout the book).

Additionally, if the remaining lease has long-term potential or has been sold and replaced by either a long-term or perpetual easement, several other elements must be considered. These include, but are not limited to:

- Is the lessee limited in future property uses by zoning, or is there a restriction specific to the use(s) outlined in the easement's governing documents (such as wireless transmission only)?

- Is the lessee responsible for property tax reimbursements? Utilities? Maintenance?

- If the lessee ceases to use or abandons the property, does the easement revert to the lessor? If so, after how long?

- Is the lessee required to remove all equipment upon departure and return the site to its previous condition (normal wear and tear excepted)?

- Is the lessee required to remove the foundation upon departure?

- Is there an expansion option?

- Who will own the tower once the lease has run its course?

- What happens if the lessee wants to install additional equipment? Is lessor permission required, or is it "by right?"

- Do subsequent lessees provide additional rent to the lessor? Check for revenue sharing, collocation, and any amendment(s).

- Have all the leases on the property been sold?

- Are there any other rights assigned in the lease sale that didn't exist in the original lease—such as expanded uses, increased tower height, etc.?

- How much will the land value of the areas (including the compound, ingress-egress easements, and utility easements) be occupied or used by the lessee(s) during their tenancy?

SELLING A CELL TOWER LEASE SEPARATELY FROM THE UNDERLYING REAL ESTATE

Lessors should take the time to understand any restrictions that may be in place and how such restrictions could affect their ability to sell the cell tower lease rights separately from the underlying real estate, especially if the lease secures the property's mortgage.

When there is a mortgage in place that includes the cell tower lease as collateral, there are four distinct scenarios that should be considered before selling the property and/or the lease:

1. The property owner seeks approval from the lender to sell the lease separately and obtains a Subordination, Non-Disturbance, and Attornment agreement (SNDA) for the benefit of the lease buyer. SNDA is defined in Chapter 4.

2. The property owner negotiates with the lender to use a portion of the proceeds from the sale of the cell tower lease to pay down or pay off the mortgage. Sometimes, lenders agree to this only if all money disbursed is used to pay down the mortgage or at least an amount equivalent to the appraised lease value. This may or may not eliminate the need for an SNDA.

3. The property owner sells the property along with the cell tower lease and lease cashflows.

4. The property owner sells the property and pays off the mortgage while retaining the lease cashflows (although the new buyer must accept the property "subject to" the cell tower lease terms).

If a property owner obtains an SNDA from the lender when the lease is executed or when the property is originally purchased (if the tower and lease were already in place), the property owner should have more control and improved flexibility with fewer complications. That said, another SNDA will likely still be required if a lease is sold to a third party.

Alternatively, suppose the tower is already constructed at the original purchase. In that case, the property owner can instruct the lender to appraise the property without the cell tower lease value and lend exclusive of the lease at the time of purchase. Such a move excludes the lease or lease payments as mortgage collateral and may unlock additional equity by completing a simultaneous lease sale during the purchase escrow. This can be complicated, so please obtain qualified cell tower lease counsel before executing any contracts.

LEASE STRIPPING

Lease Stripping is a term used to describe how a cell tower lease is separated from the underlying real estate and is either sold or held under separate ownership. If you're reading this, you probably realize that cell tower leases can be purchased and sold separately from the underlying real estate and that, if done so correctly, the process of lease stripping can create increased value for the landlord.

While not all properties or cell tower leases are candidates for lease stripping, it does not necessarily mean that lease stripping cannot (or should not) occur. It only means that the absence of the lease payments in conjunction with the remaining cell tower and associated cell tower lease may bring negative attention to the responsibilities created for the prospective property buyer when compensation is not also present and by exposing any Value Penalty.

Lease stripping can be problematic and expensive in cases in which a tower is unsightly, large, obtrusive, requires a lot of land area (such as is the case with most Guyed Towers), is located on a mid- or high-end residential property, or if the tower or tower location prevents future development or expansion according to the primary or highest and best use of the property.

A cell tower lease originally negotiated or subsequently amended inadequately can also contribute to or create a Value Penalty. For instance, the lease payments may have been too low. In the case of a low escalator, the value of the lease can become "negatively performing" (in which case, the lease may lose equity value over time because the lease escalation does not keep up with inflation.)

This can occur when a cell tower lease rent rate increases at less than market inflation (CPI). As such, it negatively affects its market sale price (and demand going forward) until a lease renegotiation opportunity presents itself or until the CPI rate falls below the escalator rate. Throughout 2022, for example, the CPI rate far outpaced the rate of most cell tower lease escalators, setting a nearly historical precedent in the industry.

Lease stripping can also be problematic based on the bundle of rights assigned to the lease buyer at the time of sale. The least restrictive form of lease stripping is a short-term sale of lease cashflows with no other leasehold interests assigned to the lease buyer. More restrictive forms of lease stripping usually involve easements and include one or more of the following clauses (which should be avoided unless compensation is adequate):

- RoFR, especially the "consent" RoFR on the property or lease sale;

- Modification or option to expand the compound area for no additional consideration;

- Expansion of the "use" clause;

- The absence of any future notice or permission requirements by the lessee(s) for upgrades or equipment additions;

- Some form of a non-complete clause on the entire underlying property to prevent the construction of another tower by a competitor on the property for the duration of the easement. This can be particularly problematic on large pieces of property.

As you can see, lease stripping is a bit of an art and, if executed correctly, should minimize or eliminate value penalty. At the same time, it should maximize a landlord's equity positions in the cell tower lease and underlying real estate.

VALUE PENALTY

Value Penalty refers to the reduction in a property's value caused by the very presence of a cell tower on a property. It does not always occur—as in the case of many commercial properties, for example—but it does happen. It becomes most obvious when a lease has been sold, and the landlord attempts to sell the property subject to the lease but without the lease cashflows.

Value Penalty will most likely occur when one or more of the following is true:

- The property is residential, single-family in nature or use (especially mid- to high-end properties);

- If the bundle of rights included in the lease hinders the property use, enjoyment, or development;

- If the land area occupied by the lease and/or tower is significant relative to the property size;

- If the tower and/or associated equipment is visibly unsightly;

- If the lifetime value of the lease's potential income is low relative to the opportunity costs.

Many brokers and sellers assume they can subtract the value of the lease from the total value of the lease and property combined and arrive at a net value for the property subject to the lease. Let me tell you, that is not often the case.

For example: Let's assume you own a single-family residential property on an acre and receive $1,000 monthly for your cell tower lease from Verizon (with no subtenants). The lease has a 3 percent annual escalator, is in the third of five 5-year options, and the tower and equipment occupy 10,000 square feet of land in the rear corner. Let's say you sold the lease to Crown Castle as a perpetual easement (with a RoFR and a non-compete) for $225,000 and would now like to sell the property separately. The property would be worth $500,000 with no cell tower. Do you think the same property with a cell tower but no lease cashflows is still worth $500,000? Likely not. The value of a property is generally higher with no cell tower and no lease cashflows than the same property is with a cell tower and no lease cashflows.

To assess the value of the property accurately, one must consider the property type, land area, tower type and height, tower compound area relative to the total land area of the property, property tax reimbursements (if any), zoning, utilities, effects on future development potential, and more. In the above-outlined case, since the cell tower occupies nearly 25 percent of the land area, it should make quite a difference if no money comes in and the lease has been sold.

In many cases, a cell tower can actually harm a property's value. However, the value penalty is not usually as obvious when the lease income is still factored into the property's total value.

Who among us likes looking at cell towers? No one I know, but cell towers will be tolerated for a price. It is largely up to the local real estate market (at the time of sale) to decide just how much the presence of a cell tower will reduce the value of the property based merely on its presence or whether the cell tower will have any effect on a given property's value at all.

The value penalty will be most dramatic on high-value residential properties, on properties that give up a great deal of land or building space for the tower's construction (thereby creating opportunity costs), in cases when a tower is very unsightly, or if the tower has been constructed in an inconvenient location that can be detrimental to future expansion/development of the property.

As mentioned previously, not all properties will suffer from a Value Penalty. For example, there are old industrial spaces in which the tower tenant is paying market value (or more) for a ground lease of just 2,500 square feet of land located on a 20-acre parcel, and for which the 2,500 square feet of leased land has no higher and better use because the tower is located out of the way in a remote part of the property, and the leased parcel is small relative to the overall property size.

But that can change. For example, when the tower tenant is paying substantially less than market rent with a below-average escalator for the tower lease (and many years remaining in the lease) or when the tower is constructed on the front of a property (which also happens to be located on a major thoroughfare or at a major intersection), and the dirt is prime redevelopment land. In the latter case, the mere presence of the cell tower could create a huge value penalty, not just from its presence and location but also from the opportunity costs involved.

Unfortunately, there are few real estate brokers, landlords, appraisers, or investors who understand the finer points of cell towers or cell tower leases, how to value them, what bundle of rights should be sold, and how to determine the consequences or benefits of a cell tower lease to a given property's value. As stated previously, cell tower leases are unique to other areas of real estate. Quite simply, there are components of a cell tower lease that are just not considered by most people when evaluating fee-simple property or commercial real estate leases.

While there are countless examples of properties listed for sale subject to a cell tower lease, it does not mean that such a sale— independent of the lease—is the best way to go, nor that it will provide the greatest profit to the seller.

Landlords are advised to seek the qualified guidance of local real estate professionals and a qualified and experienced consultant to examine and evaluate the cell tower lease and property to determine the best sales method—whether the property and lease are sold together or separately.

ENVIRONMENTAL CONCERNS

For years, real estate experts and health professionals have been making efforts to establish and better define the potentially adverse health effects that cell tower transmissions may cause to people residing in properties closely proximate to cell towers. Beyond that, many still question the financial impacts associated with such environmental concerns. While such theories and adverse effects are worthy of exploration, Lease Stripping and Value Penalty (as discussed throughout this book) are concepts that may help quantify environmental impacts in a given market at a specific time. That said, those concerns—while worthy of examination—are beyond the intended scope of this book.

If you require assistance with capitalization, monetization, management, consulting, or any other cell tower lease-related issues, please visit SteepSteel.com and submit a request to contact you for a prompt reply.

.

CHAPTER 9
CELL TOWER LEASE
MANAGEMENT FUNDAMENTALS

While the sales of cell tower leases are the holy grail for many people, the management of cell tower leases is often what it takes to reach that pinnacle. From the beginning, one must pay close attention to detail, as that is where fortunes are made and lost in the industry.

Cell tower lease management is where unforgivable mistakes are made regarding extensions, amendments, approvals, etc. It's how a significant transfer of American wealth between the private and government sectors and carriers and tower companies occurred in the past two-plus decades. Make sure you understand what not to do.

This chapter exposes the nuances of the wireless industry management from the landlord's perspective. Landlords will learn how they have been (or could be) duped.

THE DOS AND DON'TS

Cell tower leases are like other NNN ("triple net") commercial leases. However, in many ways, they are still different from leases found elsewhere in commercial or residential real estate. In this chapter, when I reference the "lessee," understand that I am speaking of carrier or tower company tenants only (they are the most sophisticated of cell tower lessees).

Keeping that in mind, one must first consider the disparity in understanding between the cell tower lessor and the cell tower lessee. For instance, while the lessor may understand the underlying real estate (or may not)—including zoning, land value, etc.—

128

the lessee often better understands the wireless infrastructure to be installed on the site and its costs, the proprietary lease, lease values in their local market, alternative sites, *and* all that the lessor knows about the underlying real estate.

When first negotiating a new wireless telecom lease, it is safe to assume that the lessor will be at a negotiating disadvantage relative to the prospective lessee (especially if the lessor is not professionally represented). After all, the prospective lessee will better understand their needs, the benefits a given site will provide, what they are willing to pay, and what alternate sites will cost.

Please remember that the cell tower lease market is opaque, unlike commercial or residential real estate. There are no comps or published rents to gauge an "appropriate" rent and escalator, revenue sharing, sub-leasing rights, etc.

While a carrier or tower company may enjoy many advantages relative to the lessor when the lease is executed, that will likely not remain the case throughout the lease life cycle. If it does, the lessor is doing something wrong.

Without delving too much into the rationale, suffice it to say that understanding each of the following management criteria is critical to minimizing lessor-lessee knowledge disparity and minimizing the likelihood that a lessee will continue to enjoy the same degree of advantage as time goes by. The following four sections discuss the categories to which one should pay close attention:

ORGANIZATION AND RECORDS

The lessor must maintain exceptional records of all lease-related documents, whether the tower is new or the property is purchased with the tower in place. This should include but not be limited to:

- Payment history (including escalation dates)

- Lease amendments, extensions, other requests or communications (including equipment upgrades), and copies of emails

- Structural engineering, surveys, and construction drawings ("CDs") for the new tower and all equipment changes or amendments

- Site photos upon installation and periodically throughout the lease life cycle, including when known equipment changes occur; such photos should include the tower, the ground equipment (including any utility meters observed), and carrier and/or tower company signage (as applicable)

- Dimensions of lease equipment compound and/or shelter(s) (as applicable)

- Copies of building permits for all permitted construction at the site

- Notes of any discrepancies observed and any associated communications as a result

A comprehensive file including the above-outlined items will reduce the advantage a given lessee might otherwise enjoy. This will come in handy during requests for amendments, upgrades, etc. It will also prove useful, should the lease mature into the final five to ten years, to effectively negotiate an extension or new lease or when selling the lease with or without the property.

SITE AND EQUIPMENT AUDITS

While a lessor may not feel comfortable performing a site and equipment audit, one should occur at least annually (or when any requests for modification are received or observed). The collection and maintenance of the data outlined in the previous section of this chapter will be helpful when the time for an audit is at hand. A cell tower lease consultant should be able to assist where and when necessary.

LOCAL REAL ESTATE

A well-informed lessor should pay close attention to local real estate prices when the lease is negotiated (if possible) and throughout the lease life cycle. Doing so will provide an improved understanding of market rents and their changes.

While this is only one variable and not *necessarily* indicative of market rent changes, it is another data point. It will help a lessor determine if the proposed rents or rent increases upon amendment or extension are appropriate or if such proposed rents create an increased potential for a "Value Penalty."

Suppose it turns out that the rents offered with any amendments or extensions do not create at least an equal increase in lease sale value as the surrounding market has increased (when considering opportunity costs). In that case, it may be appropriate to consider terminating the lease (or at least threatening to do so). That may be a better alternative than extending or authorizing an increase in ground space or equipment to the lessee in exchange for a below-market rent increase. Such a decision, however, can be complicated, so be sure to consult a cell tower lease consultant before moving forward.

NEARBY TOWERS

It's a good idea to keep a periodic watch on local cell tower development, whether through online resources or in person. One needs only examine tower locations within a few miles of a given site to understand how adjacent sites may impact the value of an already constructed site.

When keeping track of local cell towers as they are developed, building permits for known and pending sites are helpful (often available from local building departments), and carrier lessees for each site—which are available online or at the site—are also helpful.

I also recommend that cell tower lessors contact other cell tower lessors in the local market area to compare notes.

In Appendix A, there is a list of industry websites that will be useful when evaluating a cell site and the local cell tower market.

DIFFERENT INFRASTRUCTURE TYPES

In addition to the above management considerations, if a cell tower lease governs a rooftop installation or a water tower, the list of considerations outlined in the rest of this chapter should be helpful. While there are other types of wireless infrastructure, the scope of this book is intended only to consider the most common types of installations that currently exist in the U.S. marketplace.

Rooftop Installations

In many respects, rooftop antenna are like elevated water towers. However, in addition to the ongoing security and access concerns shared by both water towers and rooftops, rooftops are particularly vulnerable to damage—that may or may not be obvious—from equipment installation and subsequent changes or upgrades.

Damage concerns are not limited to the roof compound areas, as conduits and other easement areas could also be affected. That's true whether they are located on the rooftop, on the side of the building (as applicable), on the ground next to the building (as applicable), in any interior rooms that are being used for lessee equipment, or anywhere that connections exist between the areas where lessee equipment may be installed.

One should visually inspect the roof at least monthly for signs of damage. Also, if the lessee shows up to perform modifications or manage the installation, it's advisable to examine the roof once they complete their work.

Water Towers

While rooftop installations create potential problems with the roof and all connecting areas, including security, water tower installations create concerns with penetrations on the tank, the tank framing or supports, maintenance, and access.

Water tanks, like rooftops, were not usually designed to have carrier or tower company equipment installed on them. Whether it be the structural engineering, the climbing, or the potential for damage to a critical infrastructure asset required to serve the population of the given jurisdiction, most water tanks are primarily designed to hold and distribute water.

An additional consideration for water tanks and water towers is routine maintenance (including rust and corrosion removal, structural repairs, and painting) that may require the removal of lessee equipment to perform. The scheduling of any maintenance and painting should be contemplated before lease execution or before lease amendment/extension. The lessor may have to bear such equipment removal and replacement costs unless the parties otherwise agree to alternate terms at the time of lease execution, extension, or amendment.

COMPLEX TOWERS AND SITES

Beyond the aforementioned infrastructure types, it is important to note that some towers, rooftop installations, water towers, and sites—while not necessarily obvious to the casual observer—are much more complex because of the following:

- Number of tower transfers, owners, or managers

- Number of towers at a given location

- Number and nature of amendments or consents

- Combination of ground and tower leases

- The management standards and methods for any tower or site are often much different from traditional real estate with respect to value creation, risk, and ongoing development.

The above variables can make an otherwise straightforward site very difficult to manage as time progresses. To make matters worse, the more transfers, owners, or managers that exist in the history of a site, the more difficult it becomes to maintain accurate and adequate records, as few landlords are familiar with transfer documents, and keep an organized record of pertinent documents for years or decades.

Beyond these items, I have observed that the more owners, managers, and transfers in a given site's history, the more likely errors associated with amendments, extensions, payments, escalations, and reimbursements occur, and such errors typically become cumulative.

TAKEAWAY: PLEASE DO NOT ATTEMPT TO MANAGE A COMPLEX TOWER OR SITE WITHOUT PROFESSIONAL ASSISTANCE.

CHAPTER 10
PRACTICAL DIFFERENCES BETWEEN VARIOUS TOWER INSTALLATION TYPES AND THEIR ASSOCIATED AGREEMENTS

The obvious distinction between a ground-based cell tower and a rooftop installation is that a tower is most often constructed on the ground, while a rooftop installation is constructed atop a building or on another similar structure. Having wireless infrastructure on the roof of one's building is entirely different from having a cell tower at the corner of one's property and should be treated as such.

DIFFERENCES BETWEEN GROUND-BASED CELL TOWERS AND ROOFTOP INSTALLATIONS

Rooftop installations and ground-based towers (as well as associated lease or license documents) have numerous similarities and differences.

For example:

Ground-based towers are usually located directly adjacent to their ground-based equipment and backup generators in a single leased/easement area, often with other easements to provide site access and utilities.

The same cannot be said for rooftop installations. There are many examples of rooftop installations on roofs of buildings where the associated equipment is installed somewhere on the ground next to the building and/or in a room, or rooms, within the building.

LEASE VERSUS LICENSE

Considering the significant installation and access requirements required for rooftop installations, I recommend that licenses—as opposed to leases—be used as the basis for rooftop agreements with any carrier or tower company.

The rationale is that licenses are not always assignable to a third party, will not confer any interest in the property, will not provide exclusive possession to the licensee, and will provide the licensor greater control over the property and the licensee than would be the case with a lease.

CONTROL AND SUBLICENSEES

Tower companies often seek to control the entire rooftop, or most of the rooftop (as well as all pertinent portions of the building), for their equipment and antenna. However, they may only use a fraction of the roof for a single tenant. I don't recommend agreeing to this unless the compensation package reduces opportunity costs and minimizes value penalties.

This approach often means a yearly option fee for additional space is negotiated, and revenue share is in place if the initial licensee delivers subsequent licensees. Any such sublicensees should provide guaranteed rent minimums and escalations.

It is advantageous for the building owner to reserve a portion of the rooftop for any prospective second, third, and subsequent licensees who may attempt to make a direct inquiry with the building owner about collocating on the roof. Such inquiries directly to a building owner are quite common.

I also recommend that if a prospective additional rooftop licensee contacts the licensor directly (for which the initial licensee is not the procuring cause), the licensor licenses a portion of the rooftop; as a result, no revenue share should be due to the initial licensee. Any revenue share to the original licensee would only be due if the initial license is the procuring cause for any subsequent licensees, the license provides sublicensee rights to the original licensee, or if the existing licensee is paying an annual option fee in addition to their rent.

SITE CONFIGURATION AND USE

Antenna placement should be inside the building parapet (or otherwise hidden/disguised from view) whenever possible. The placement of antenna should not detract from the building architecture (see Value Penalty). Rooftop antenna installations are ideally hidden from view.

There may be multiple easements and license areas for a rooftop installation wherein one (or more) will be on the rooftop for the antenna or equipment. Another may be for cables, utility wires, poles, conduits, and pipes that connect the rooftop antenna with transmission equipment (perhaps on the ground or inside the building). Others will be for ingress and egress over, upon, through, and/or across the parking area, building, common areas, stairways, elevators, driveways, conduits, shafts, risers, or other property features.

Be aware that the carrier or tower company may (inadvertently) underestimate the size of the easements and license areas relative to what is ultimately constructed on the rooftop. The result is that, in many cases, the carrier or tower company will gain additional space (that is virtually unnoticeable to the licensor) but will provide room for additional equipment, antenna, or a generator at little to no additional expense to the licensee. The dimensions of all areas are critical on a rooftop, as are all easements running between the rooftop, the building interior or exterior, and the ground.

INSPECTIONS AND AUDITS

Annual site audits should be performed to verify consistency between the lease compound, the easement areas, all conduits, equipment verification, and anything else that might create an opportunity to be exploited by licensees or their vendors.

All equipment changes or upgrades on a roof should require an amendment and a rent increase for any additional space outside the original compound or easement areas. Also, suppose the license does not permit changes in equipment by right or any increase in the number of equipment cabinets. In that case, any increase in the dimensions of antenna, cables, connectors, wires, radios, radio shelters, or related transmission or reception hardware or software may create an opportunity for the licensor to seek a rent increase. The same may also be true for any increase in capacity or weight.

DAMAGE AND REPAIRS

Unlike ground-based towers, where the primary lessor-owned areas that might sustain damage are often limited to landscaping and pavement (absent a tower fall), installing antenna and associated equipment on rooftops can cause damage to building systems. The terms for repair and liability must be spelled out carefully.

TERMINOLOGY

Be cognizant of license terminology variation in rooftop installations (especially relative to ground-based towers). Carriers and tower companies may use a mix of similarly sounding/looking terms within the same license, but those terms may have different meanings. Here are some examples:

- Premises

- Licensed Premises

- Licensed Area

- New Licensed Area

- Existing Licensed Premises

- Property

- Building

- Rooftop

- Rooftop License Area

- New Licensee

- Licensee

- Replacement Licensee

- Rooftop Licensees

- New Licensee Revenue

- Replacement License Revenue

- Replacement License

- Rooftop Tenant Licenses

- and so on.

SECURITY

Building security should also be spelled out carefully from the beginning of the planning and development process to the end of the lease. Some buildings with rooftop installations are high-security and may require additional or enhanced considerations or precautions because of the 24/7 emergency access required by carriers and tower companies.

The license terms should also include a security protocol that outlines access restrictions and requirements when any carrier, tower company, employees, or vendors visit the site for initial installation, repair, replacement, maintenance, upgrades, or emergencies.

Ensure that the roof is engineered to support the weight of the equipment before any rooftop installation. Equipment weight may exceed the engineered weight limit of the roof. To determine this, contact a structural engineer or request any potential licensee to do so and provide you with a structural analysis at the licensee's expense.

If the building is not designed to support the weight of a rooftop installation, make certain that any new licensee is willing to pay for and make the necessary structural changes as a part of the license terms before installing any equipment.

Rooftop installations can become intrusive. Therefore, all surveys, engineering, and construction drawings must be completed and approved before license execution. A professional review of all such documents is highly recommended. It may be quite costly (which should immediately be passed on to the prospective licensee during the application and negotiation process).

ROOFTOP MAINTENANCE

Designing a pre-construction rooftop installation, maintenance, and security protocol should be negotiated into the license and may include the following considerations:

- **Development of a controlled 24-hour access plan.** Because the licensee(s) will require 24/7/365 access, procedures and routes often require advanced planning.

- **Building inspection and repairs.** These must be performed before and after construction, and all affected areas should be inspected. After all, some degree of repair work is to be expected.

- **Periodic inspections.** Unlike a ground-based tower, rooftop installations require regular, periodic inspections to ensure nothing is unsightly damaged or showing signs of wear. Special inspections will also be required after major weather events or when equipment additions, upgrades, or swap-outs occur.

Finally, the square footage required for installing rooftop equipment (as well as occasional ground/interior equipment) and the cabling/conduit requirements for that equipment are greater than for equivalent ground-based tower installations. That may increase opportunity and maintenance costs to the licensor. Therefore, rents for a rooftop installation should be greater than similar rents for a ground-based installation, especially when the carrier or tower company will not be required to construct a tower and will save a significant portion of financial investment in the process.

WATER TANKS & WATER TOWERS

Water towers (a.k.a. raised or elevated water tanks) and ground-based water tanks are designed primarily to pump, hold, and drain large quantities of water, usually for government agencies on behalf of the local public. They make great short-term telecom solutions but are far from ideal in the long-term.

While carriers and tower companies have been using water towers and water tanks as *de facto* cell towers for decades, and government agencies and utilities have largely allowed it and have cooperated with licensees to allow access to ground and tower equipment, it's not always a happy marriage.

Like rooftop installations, it's advantageous for landlords to negotiate a license instead of a lease for any prospective wireless tenants seeking to occupy a water tower or any adjacent ground space.

Unfortunately, it has been discovered over time that cell tower infrastructure and water tanks contain inherent conflicts of purpose that can create problems. These conflicts often include:

- **Access:** Most water tanks and towers are considered critical infrastructure government agencies operate. As such, access is tightly restricted. Unfortunately, licensees often require 24-hour, 7-day-per-week access, which can create problems.

- **Maintenance:** Water tanks require routine maintenance. That can interfere with carrier or tower company operations, especially if licensee equipment removal is required, which is often the case.

- **Removal and Replacement:** One can expect that carrier equipment may require removal and replacement at least once every fifteen to twenty years. How often depends on the maintenance schedule, the climate of the water tank, the type of maintenance being performed, and the placement of the equipment on the water tank. This should be considered at the time a lease is negotiated. Otherwise, the tank owner may be forced to bear the removal and replacement costs, which can cost upward of $100,000 or more in some cases. The cost of removal and replacement depends on the number of licensees, the amount of their installed equipment, and whether a "Cell-site On Wheels" ("C.O.W.") or similar installation is required.

- **Useful Life:** Currently, there are thousands of water tanks around the U.S. with carrier or tower company equipment mounted atop and/or on the sides. Many of these tanks are decades old and are in less-than-perfect shape. Aging can lead to structural problems that may force a water tank to be decommissioned and the carrier or tower company equipment to be forced off. The age and condition of the tank must be considered before entering a license with a carrier or tower company, and the terms should be negotiated accordingly.

UTILITY-OWNED TRANSMISSION TOWERS

Just as with water towers, transmission towers are likely considered critical infrastructure. They are less than ideal for wireless telecom but for different reasons than water tanks and towers. In the case of transmission towers, it is not the tower itself that poses problems.

Issues with transmission towers are more likely associated with the complexity of creating and managing multi-party leases between a government agency or private landlord, a utility provider, and a carrier or tower company. After all, the needs of each of the parties are not likely synchronized (or even aligned), which will likely create a few conflicts during a long-term lease life cycle.

If a lessor has a utility tower on their property and a lessee requires only a ground lease for the equipment, revenue share, and collocation rights can become more complex. The carrier or tower company may also have a separate tower lease with the utility company.

In the above cases, it should be understood by the lessor that tower "alternatives" (such as water and transmission towers)—while potentially solving problems on the front end of a lease—will likely contribute to future problems that should be anticipated and negotiated well in advance.

CHAPTER 11
CELL TOWER LEASE SALE TYPES AND
POTENTIAL TAX IMPLICATIONS

This chapter covers some details about cell tower lease sales previously covered in Chapter 5. However, this chapter's context, considerations, and applications are different.

CELL TOWER LEASE SALE STRUCTURES

Most people aren't aware that there is more than one way to sell and transfer the rights to a cell tower lease. Generally, cell tower lease sale structures fall into two distinct categories, each with its rights, considerations, and potential consequences. These categories are:

Conversion to an Easement – Depending on the duration of the lease, the lessor will assign the remaining lease rights (and, often, the successor lease rights), as well as the right to receive or retain the lease cash flows, and grant an easement to either the tower owner or a third party in exchange for a lump-sum payment or a series of guaranteed installments. Doing so will convert the leased areas into a term or perpetual easement upon closing.

Lease buyers often prefer easements upon sale, seeking additional rights, benefits, privileges, and even land area relative to the original lease (a.k.a. "a second bite at the apple"). Few third-party lease buyers opt to purchase a cell tower lease without including an easement to outline and secure such additional rights, benefits, and privileges. On the other hand, Tower companies may offer such an alternative on their existing sites.

147

Immediate ("Lump Sum") or Deferred Sale of Lease Cash-flows – The lessor assigns the rights to receive the future lease cash flows from the current (and, often, the successor lease) to the lease tenant or tower owner in exchange for a lump-sum payment or payments payable in guaranteed installments over several years. Installment sales are also considered a viable alternative to an IRC Section 1031 tax-deferred exchange (hereinafter a "1031 exchange") by spreading the potential tax liability over several years when a 1031 Exchange may not be an option.

Most often, in the case of a lump sum or installment sale of lease cashflows, the simple assignment of lease cashflows should have little effect on the leased areas or the lease itself. Such assignments may serve only to change the name of the lease payee.

That's not to say that a tower company won't seek additional privileges. Some concessions may be acceptable or necessary depending on how the lease is structured and how much time remains.

In the case of an easement sale or a 1031 exchange with the lease going to a third party, the seller should expect to execute a rent redirect letter in addition to the easement and assignment of cashflow documents. That letter will notify the existing carrier(s) and/or tower company of the party to which/whom the rent should be paid subsequently.

CELL TOWER LEASE SALE DURATION OPTIONS

In a nutshell, the sale duration of cell tower leases will fall into one of two primary and distinct types (and such sales may or may not include the recordation of an easement):

> **Term** – Generally, term easements may range from a few years to ninety-nine years, with a 50-year term being about the industry average. The 99-year term easement was a solution to restrictions against perpetual easements

enacted in some states. Correctly or incorrectly, these are often seen as a solution to the "rule against perpetuities" in some states. Many argue that such legislation eliminates de facto subdivisions by a perpetual easement, thereby sidestepping a state's subdivision map laws (and local zoning ordinances) by assigning a bundle of rights to a non-fee owner for a greater period than twenty-one years beyond a natural lifetime.

Perpetual – This term refers to selling cell tower lease rights or cashflows for over ninety-nine years. It almost always occurs in conjunction with a recorded easement and an assignment of the lease. The sale of a lease converted to an easement in perpetuity will often achieve the greatest price received relative to all other lease sale types or duration.

CELL TOWER LEASE SALE AND INCOME TAX CONSIDERATIONS

In addition to the above lease sale structure and term considerations, a seller of a cell tower lease should consider potential income tax consequences and solutions. Another consideration should be the tax benefits associated with a 1031 Exchange. However, there are many formal requirements, all of which must be satisfied to qualify under Section 1031 for a tax-deferred exchange.

For instance, a 1031 Exchange requires the use of an authorized "exchange facilitator," who will act to receive funds from the first escrow upon sale of the cell tower lease (the "relinquished property" in this example) and distribute the funds to the up-leg escrow for the purchase of the "replacement property."

Beyond the sale structure, one must be cognizant of tax planning to minimize the payment of legally required income taxes once a cell tower lease is sold. A seller may also want to consider how to structure a 1031 Exchange (before such a sale) to avoid some or all potential income taxes that might otherwise become due. One should consider several things before a potential cell tower lease sale as part of a detailed tax-planning strategy when determining the feasibility of a 1031 Exchange. These considerations include, but are not limited to, the following:

Like-kind replacement property: If one is anticipating the sale of a cell tower lease as a part of a 1031 Exchange, it must be for another real property (whether commercial or residential), and the lease sale must be recorded on the relinquished property title as an easement.

Duration of hold: While many people assume that, to qualify for a 1031 exchange, the relinquished property must be held for twelve months, that is not the case.

Qualified-use test: The relinquished property on which the lease is located cannot be the seller's primary residence but instead must be a property held for use in a trade or business or for investment. The same is true for the replacement property.

Replacement property: Many people are unaware of the timelines associated with the 1031 Exchange. IRC Section 1031 requires identifying potential like-kind replacement properties within 45 days after the sale of the relinquished property (the "identification period") and closing on a replacement property purchase within 180 days after the sale of the relinquished property (the "exchange period"). IRC Section 1031 typically allows up to three prospective properties to be identified as replacement prospects (though, apparently, there is no official limit).

Intent to hold: The facts surrounding the sale and the seller's subsequent actions may be examined by taxing authorities to determine if an exchange is invalid. One noteworthy case is *Goolsby v. Comm'r T.C. Memo 2010-64 (April 1, 2010)*. Suppose the IRS determines insufficient intent to hold the relinquished or replacement property for trade, business, or investment purposes. In that case, a seller may be liable for paying capital gains taxes. Negligence penalties and interest may also be applied.

Duration and Type of Sale: The IRS has issued at least one PLR ("Private Letter Ruling") indicating that, to meet the "like-kind" test for the exchange of a cell tower lease into fee-simple real estate, a minimum of a 30-year easement of the relinquished property is required.

Acquisition Cost: The replacement property must have an acquisition cost equal to or greater than the adjusted sale price of the relinquished property.

Mortgage Debt: Any new mortgage debt obtained with the purchase of the replacement property should be equal to or greater than the debt paid off for the relinquished property, or new cash may be required to offset any difference.

Cash Retention: Any cash the seller retains from the relinquished property proceeds may be subject to tax exposure.

As an example, the IRS issued Private Letter Ruling 201149003, dated August 31, 2011 (hereinafter "IRS PLR 201149003"),

which is not "legal authority" but is instructive as to the IRS's legal position; the IRS held in favor of the taxpayer. The case is summarized as follows (with a complete copy of the original Ruling available in PDF at
https://www.irs.gov/pub/irs-wd/1149003.pdf):

Facts

The Taxpayer is a newly formed State X corporation that currently holds no assets, has no operations, and has not been elected under subchapter M, part II, of the Code to be treated for federal income tax purposes as a real estate investment trust (REIT).

The Taxpayer proposes to engage in the business of acquiring, owning, and leasing certain easements (Easements) in, to, under, and over certain real property (Properties) and to elect to be treated for federal income tax purposes as a REIT.

Company A, Company B, Company C, and "Management Group," a group of natural persons who are involved in the management of LLC 1, collectively own a percentage of LLC 1. The equity interest of Company A, Company B, Company C, and Management Group in LLC1 is b percent, c percent, d percent, and e percent, respectively.

A percent of the Taxpayer is owned by LLC 1. LLC 1 also owns a percentage of the membership interests in LLC 2. LLC 2 owns a percent of the membership interests in LLC 3. LLC 3 owns a percent of the membership interests in LLC 5 and LLC 6.

LLC 1 also holds a percent of the membership interest in LLC 4. LLC 4 holds a percent of the membership interests in LLC 7 and LLC 8. In addition to owning the membership interests in LLC 7 and LLC 8, LLC 4 holds various other entity interests and investments.

LLC 5, LLC 6, LLC 7, and LLC 8 (collectively, the "Current Easement Holders") are presently engaged in the business of acquiring, owning, and leasing Easements over Properties. The Taxpayer represents that the details of this business are as described below.

Before the Easement is created, the owner of the Property (Owner) enters into at least one lease agreement regarding the Property (Lease) with a wireless communication provider (Lessee). The Lessee enters into the Lease to install towers, antenna, buildings, fences, gates, and other equipment and facilities in connection with its wireless communication business (each, a "Cell Phone Tower"). Taxpayer represents the following is a summary of the principal terms of a typical Lease and that these terms are representative of the terms of all Leases:

Parties. The Owner and the Lessee.

Leased Site. The Owner leases to the Lessee a portion of the Property consisting of f square feet, including air space above such area and access to the nearest public road (the "Site").

Permitted Use. The Lessee is permitted to use the Site for the transmission and reception of communications signals and the installation, maintenance and operation, repair, and replacement of communications fixtures on a g foot monopole and related equipment, cables, accessories, and improvements, which may include a support structure, antenna, equipment shelters or cabinets, fencing, and other items necessary to the successful use of the Site.

Term. The initial term of a Lease is h years, which will automatically renew for h additional periods of h years each unless the Lessee notifies the Owner in writing at least 1 day prior to the expiration of the current h-year period.

Rent. During the first year of the term of the Lease, the Lessee is required to pay $j per month in rent to the Owner. During the second and subsequent years, the amount of rent will increase by k percent over the amount of rent in the previous year. The Lessee has the right to sublet part of the Site for additional communications facilities, with the consent of the Owner. In the event of such a sublease, the Lessee will pay the Owner l percent of the rent received by the Lessee from the sublease as additional rent under the Lease.

Termination. The Lease may be terminated by either party on m days' written notice if the other party remains in default (see below) after the applicable cure periods.

Default. The Lessee will be deemed to be in default if (1) The Lessee fails to pay rent for more than n days after receipt of written notice from the Owner, or (2) The Lessee fails to perform any other term or condition of the Lease within m days after receipt of written notice by the Owner. However, no default will be deemed as long as the Lessee has begun to cure the default within the specified period and provided that such efforts are prosecuted to completion with reasonable diligence.

The Current Easement Holders enter into agreements with Owners with respect to the Properties (Easement Agreements). The Taxpayer represents the Easement Agreements, which are the agreements the Taxpayer will use when it engages in the business of acquiring, owning, and leasing Easements. Pursuant to the terms of each Easement Agreement, the Owner grants the Easement Holder the Easement, which consists of the following:

(1) An exclusive easement over a portion of the Property that includes the Site and Cell Phone Tower (Exclusive Easement); and

(2) Non-exclusive easements over areas that are necessary for (a) ingress to and egress from the Exclusive Easement and a pub-

licly dedicated roadway, (b) installation, repair, replacement, improvement, maintenance, and removal of utilities providing service to the Exclusive Easement and the Cell Phone Tower, and (c) for Sites located on building rooftops, access to building risers, conduits, shafts, raceways, or other designated space to connect the Lessee's equipment to other locations in the building.

Additionally, the Owner transfers and assigns to the Current Easement Holder all rights, titles, and interests of the Owner in the Leases. Accordingly, the Current Easement Holder takes the Easements subject to the Leases, becoming the landlord under each Lease, assuming responsibility for all of the obligations and liabilities of the Owner, and receiving the Rent that the Lessee otherwise would have paid to the Owner. The only obligations of the Owner under the Lease that are not assigned to the Current Easement Holder are obligations relating to the ownership, operation, and use of the Property.

The Current Easement Holder has the unrestricted right to lease, license, transfer, or assign, in whole or in part to, or permit the use of the Easements and/or its rights under the Easement Agreement by any third parties, including communication service providers or tower owners or operators, including the Lessee. Often, the Lessee will sublease the Site and Cell Phone Tower to a sublessee (Sublessee), and the Sublessee will need space in addition to the Site for the performance of its duties under the sublease. In these cases, the Sublessee may request that the Current Easement Holder lease a portion of the Easement outside the Site.

Upon the expiration of the Lease, the Current Easement Holder may enter into a new lease of its rights with respect to the Property with any third party. Even before the expiration of a Lease, the Current Easement Holder may enter into a new lease of a portion of its rights with respect to the Property to the extent it is not subject to a Lease.

Most Easement Agreements and Easements are perpetual in duration as long as the Easements remain in use, but the Easement Agreement will terminate, and the Easements will expire if the Easements are abandoned for more than h years for reasons other than casualty, condemnation, or act of God. A small number of Easement Agreements and Easements are long-term but not perpetual in duration, generally about m to o years.

In consideration of the foregoing, the Current Easement Holder pays the Owner a purchase price based on a fixed amount with some contingent elements.

Taxpayer anticipates that the Current Easement Holders will transfer the Easements to Taxpayer and that Taxpayer will thereafter engage in the business of acquiring, owning, and leasing the existing Easements received from the Current Easement Holders as well as new Easements and elect to be treated as a REIT for federal income tax purposes.

Conclusion

Based on the information submitted and representations made, we conclude that (1) an Easement acquired by the Taxpayer under an Easement Agreement is "an interest in real property" that qualifies under § 856(c)(5)(B) as a "real estate asset," and (2) the amounts derived by the Taxpayer under the terms of Easement Agreements pursuant to the Leases are "rents from real property" within the meaning of § 856(d)(1).

This ruling's application is limited to the facts, representations, Code sections, and regulations cited herein. Except as specifically ruled upon above, no opinion is expressed concerning any federal income tax consequences relating to the facts herein under any other provision of the Code. Specifically, we do not rule on the following: (1) whether the Taxpayer otherwise qualifies as a REIT under part II of subchapter M of Chapter 1 of the Code, and (2) the federal tax consequences of the transaction or series of transactions by which the existing Easements will be transferred, contributed, assigned, or otherwise conveyed from the Current Easement Holders to the Taxpayer.

This ruling is directed only to the taxpayer who requested it. Section 6110(k)(3) provides that it may not be used or cited as precedent. In accordance with the Power of Attorney on file with this office, a copy of this letter is being sent to your authorized representatives.

CONVERSION OF 1031 EXCHANGE REAL PROPERTY INTO REITS

Some attorneys specialize in the conversion of real property assets into REITs by first converting the real property assets into shares of a Delaware Statutory Trust ("DST"), then converting ownership of the DST shares into Operating Partnership (OP) units through an umbrella Partnership Real Estate Investment Trust (UPREIT).

This process may allow cell tower lessors to monetize and exchange the lease equity into American Tower, Crown Castle, or SBA shares (although the process can be time-consuming). Such tower company stocks have performed far better than most annual or periodic lease escalators during the past ten years. For example, American Tower has delivered an average increase in value of about 15 percent (excluding dividends) since 2012 (despite its poor performance in 2022).

ADDITIONAL CONSIDERATIONS

In addition to the above considerations about cell tower lease sale structures and durations, one should recognize that if the relinquished property is in the form of an easement for at least thirty years in duration, while it will likely qualify for a 1031 Exchange, the sale may not qualify for *long-term capital gains tax treatment* unless the relinquished property has also been held for at least one year.

It should also be noted that, per IRS PLR 201149003, even if the cell tower lease being relinquished meets all of the other legally required conditions of a 1031 Exchange, if the sale includes the cell tower lease cashflows only (and is not recorded as an easement), the IRS may not consider the sale as "like-kind." If not, it would result in the IRS invalidating the exchange, thus creating significant unanticipated tax expenses for the seller.

The above-outlined examples are not exhaustive concerning the transaction types or the tax laws that may apply in a given scenario.

Depending on the complexity of the proposed cell tower lease-related 1031 Exchange, one might also want to seek the advice of a qualified tax professional to request the issuance of a Private Letter Ruling from the IRS (per IRS Rev. Proc. 2011-1) before entering a contract to sell a cell tower lease. There appears to be little else in the way of IRS PLRs or tax court rulings concerning the sale of cell tower leases as a part of a 1031 Exchange. However, many professionals in the wireless telecommunications industry insist that IRS PLR 201149003 has been a well-accepted basis for 1031 Exchanges since publication. If a sale occurs under substantially different circumstances than those outlined in IRS PLR 201149003, the outcome may be different. That may lead to potential unforeseen taxes, penalties, and interest.

SPECIAL ISSUES FOR GOVERNMENT AGENCIES AND NON-PROFITS

For local and state government agencies, public utilities, public schools, colleges, and universities (all tax-exempt), cell tower lease sales rules are quite different from those for their private sector or for-profit counterparts. Most government and non-profit entities enjoy tax-free status and are rarely subject to income or property tax obligations.

That said, it's important to note that, in some states, the sale of a cell tower lease by a tax-exempt government agency may trigger a possessory interest in real property and could become subject to property taxation. The property tax could—in theory—become a liability for the selling (and otherwise tax-exempt) agency unless other terms are negotiated as a part of the cell tower lease sale before transaction consummation.

Finally, in the case of non-profits, the income derived from selling a cell tower lease may be subject to ordinary income tax if the rents paid under the lease were historically subject to income taxes. If the rental income was previously considered to be derived from "unrelated business activities" and subject to "unrelated business income tax," then the lease sale may create an income tax consequence often referred to as an "acceleration of ordinary income."

If you require assistance with capitalization, monetization, management, consulting, or any other cell tower lease-related issues, please visit SteepSteel.com and submit a request to contact you for a prompt reply.

APPENDIX A
INDUSTRY WEBSITES

MAJOR U.S. CARRIER COVERAGE MAPS

AT&T (ATT.com)
AT&T U.S. Coverage Maps (2025)
Verizon (Verizon.com)
Verizon U.S. Coverage Maps (2025)
T-Mobile (TMobile.com)
T-Mobile U.S. Coverage Maps (2025)
U.S. Cellular (USCellular.com)
U.S. Cellular U.S. Coverage Map (2025)
Dish Wireless (DishWireless.com)
Dish Wireless U.S. Coverage Map (2025)
CellularMaps.com (2025)

MAJOR U.S. TOWER COMPANIES*

Crown Castle (CrownCastle.com)
American Tower (AmericanTower.com)
SBA Communications (SBASite.com)
United State Cellular Co. (USCellular.com)
Vertical Bridge (VerticalBridge.com)
Time Warner (KGIWireless.com)
Diamond Communications (DiamondComm.com)
Phoenix Tower International (PhoenixIntnl.com)

* Not by ranking (wireless industry only – not secondary)

GOVERNMENT AGENCIES

FCC (fcc.gov)

FAA (faa.gov)
WTB (wireless.fcc.gov)
CTIA (ctia.org)

MISCELLANEOUS INDUSTRY WEBSITES

Inside Towers (insidetowers.com)
Antenna Search (antennasearch.com)
Cell Reception (cellreception.com)
Open Signal (opensignal.com)
Black Dot (blackdotwireless.com)
The Lyle Company (lyleco.com)
Md7 (md7.com)
5G Technology World (5gtechnologyworld.com)
RCR Wireless (rcrwireless.com)
Fierce Wireless (fiercewireless.com)
Fierce Telecom (fiercetelecom.com)
Wireless Estimator (wirelessestimator.com)
Telecoms (telecoms.com)
Light Reading (lightreading.com)
Unison (unisonsite.com)
TowerPro (tower-pro.com)
TIA (tiaonline.org)

APPENDIX B
TYPES OF COMMUNICATIONS TOWERS, ROOFTOP ANTENNAS, AND OTHER INFRASTRUCTURE TYPES

EXAMPLES APPEAR ON THE FOLLOWING PAGE

Flagpole

Lattice and Guyed

Lattice

Lattice Tower

Lattice

Microwave and Backhaul Repeater

Microwave Backhaul

Microwave Backhaul

Monopalm

Monopine

Monopine

Monopole

Monopole

Rooftop

Rooftop

Water Tower

Water Tower

GLOSSARY OF IMPORTANT
TERMS AND PHRASES

Lease Stripping – The process of selling or holding a cell tower lease independent of the underlying real estate.

Value Penalty – Any reduction in a property's value due to the presence of a cell tower on the property that is not more than offset by the revenue received by the lessor from the tower lease. It may also include opportunity costs and become more obvious because of Lease Stripping.

Mailbox Money – The management of a cell tower lease (or any property) wherein the primary consideration is the collection of timely rent and continued tenancy with low vacancy. For cell tower leases, lessors who only worry about "Mailbox Money" may lose sight of more important value drivers in the process, which may significantly impact the lease's rent and/or sale value for many years.

Master License Agreement ("MLA") – An agreement usually applies to several sites. Used to outline rents, escalators, cancelation terms, and other common clauses governing multiple sites while factoring in site-specific limitations or requirements. MLAs are commonly used between carriers and tower companies, carriers and carriers, or between large corporate or public landlords and carriers to tower companies.

Value Drivers – Any of several variables that may increase ("drive") a cell tower lease's rental or sale value.

Lease Optimization – Typically occurs when a lessee seeks to improve their lease terms, either the rent, the escalator, the duration, or some combination of these. Optimizations may also occur in conjunction with a lease extension.

Lease Monetization – Selling cell tower leases (with or without the real estate) to the lessee, tower owner, or a third party.

Right of First Refusal ("RoFR") – Rights of First Refusal are designed to prevent lessors from selling a lease without notice and consent by the lessee. RoFRs come in a few forms, some requiring a price match or outright permission from the lessee. RoFRs may also affect a sale of the real estate or just a sale of the lease(s).

Collocates (or "Colocates") – Collocates (typically some or all of the subtenants) occur on a large percentage of cell towers and provide a great opportunity for the lessor—depending on the lease—to receive increased rents. They also allow the tower owner to achieve large profit margins and rents that may be greater than the base ground lease rent.

Revenue Sharing – Revenue sharing is the net benefit of collocates with a properly negotiated lease. It dictates the amount the lessor receives in a split with the lessee. I have observed splits that completely favored the lessee while others favored the lessor. There are several factors to consider when such negotiations are in play.

SNDA – A subordination, non-disturbance, and attornment agreement (SNDA) addresses the priority of the tenant's rights and any lenders. It deals with how and when the rights of the lessee will be subordinate to the rights of the lenders or, sometimes at the lender's option, senior to the lender's rights.

Lease Life Cycle – The entire potential lease span (typically 25-50 years for cell tower leases). During the lease duration, as time elapses, and assuming the tower is further developed with more collocates, the leverage typically shifts from the lessee to the lessor, often creating an opportunity to negotiate large lessor upsides when extending or amending a soon-to-be-mature lease.

Non-Compete – A form of a restrictive covenant (a.k.a .an "Exclusivity" clause). For cell tower leases, the right for an existing ground lease tenant to approve and/or control whether another tower is built on the property.

Be careful with non-compete clauses. To some lessors, someone with a cell tower consuming a small portion of their 10,000-square-foot lot, for instance—a non-compete clause will not likely create an issue. After all, there is little room to add another tower on the property.

However, if you own a multi-acre parcel and a carrier or tower company slips a non-compete clause into the lease, although they may only be leasing a 5,000-square-foot portion of your 50-acre parcel, the carrier or tower company may prevent you from leasing any land to a competing carrier or tower company thereby preventing additional cell tower-related revenue opportunities.

Non-Compete clauses should be eliminated (or negotiated to the least impactful version from the landlord's perspective), if possible.

ABOUT THE AUTHOR

James Kennedy has worked in real estate investment and development for nearly thirty years. He has also been involved in cell tower lease analysis, consulting, and investment for more than twenty of those years. During that time, he has reviewed, analyzed, and negotiated thousands of cell tower leases worth hundreds of millions of dollars.

With a Master of Business Administration from the University of Southern California, a Master of Science in Real Estate from the University of Denver, and the highly-coveted Certified Commercial Investment Member ("CCIM") designation, James is uniquely qualified to analyze, interpret, critique, and discuss cell tower leases and their impact on underlying and adjacent real properties.

James has been featured in numerous wireless, real estate, and government publications, including Realtormag, Commercial Investment Real Estate, American City & County, CoStar, Institute of Real Estate Management, and the Washington Association of Sewer & Water Districts.

As Founder and CEO of SteepSteel (SteepSteel.com), James leads a highly qualified team of industry professionals to provide wireless asset management, monetization, and consulting to government agencies, utilities, corporate, and private clients around the United States. The SteepSteel team also has extensive experience with water tower-based cell sites.

www.ingramcontent.com/pod-product-compliance
Lightning Source LLC
Chambersburg PA
CBHW070421290526
45791CB00005B/1783